Fine, Ralph Adam, 1941-
    Mary Jane versus Pennsylvania: the day
the Supreme Court heard the arguments for
and against the legalization of marijuana.
New York, McCall Pub. Co. [1970]
    v, 154 p.   22cm.

    "A work of fiction set in the near
future."

    1. Marijuana.   2. Narcotic laws--U.S.
I. Title.

MARY JANE
VERSUS
PENNSYLVANIA

MARY JANE
VERSUS
PENNSYLVANIA

The Day the Supreme Court
Heard the Arguments for and against
the Legalization of Marijuana

RALPH ADAM FINE

The McCall Publishing Company

NEW YORK

To my mother and father;
Burt and Brenda;
and, of course,
Kay

Published simultaneously in Canada by
Doubleday Canada Ltd., Toronto.

Library of Congress Catalog Card Number: 77–122143

SBN: 8415–0048–7

Design by Tere LoPrete

The McCall Publishing Company
230 Park Avenue, New York, N.Y. 10017

PRINTED IN THE UNITED STATES OF AMERICA

PREFACE

Mary Jane VERSUS *Pennsylvania* is a work of fiction set in the near future. It is an account of the arguments before the United States Supreme Court of a case involving the possession of marijuana. The question posed to the Justices of the Court is whether marijuana—its possession and its use—should be made legal. The contending lawyers and, of course, all of the dialogue are fictional, but the arguments that are used on either side are based upon actual scientific experiments, studies, and reports.

Writing this book has given me the rare opportunity to argue both sides of a case through the minds of other men. I have attempted to do so with thoroughness and impartiality. Although the names of the actual sitting Justices of the Supreme Court have been changed, the legal principles at the heart of the marijuana controversy have been formulated by real men, some of whom are currently on the Court. The questions I have had the Justices ask are similar to questions that are typically asked in Supreme Court arguments and reflect my reading of what their general approach might be in this type of case.

—R. A. F.

PART ONE

The Day of the Argument

U.S. Supreme Court to Hear Marijuana Case Tomorrow

1969 Pennsylvania Ruling to Be Challenged in Proceedings that Could Lead to Legalization of Drug

By PHILIP SPITZER
Special to The New York Times

WASHINGTON, Feb. 12 —The Supreme Court will hear oral argument on Monday in a case that could open the door to the legalization of marijuana.

The case, Rodriguez v. Pennsylvania, is on appeal from the Supreme Court of Pennsylvania. It concerns Peter Rodriguez, 27 years old, of Harrisburg, who was sentenced to three years in prison —two and one half suspended —in November 1969 for illegal possession of two marijuana cigarettes. In recent months civil libertarians have been referring to the case as "Mary Jane Versus Pennsylvania" — "Mary Jane" is a slang term for marijuana.

At a press conference at the National Press Club yesterday, Jonathan N. Smith, attorney for Mr. Rodriguez, said he would argue before the Court that marijuana was not as dangerous as the Commonwealth of Pennsylvania contended and that laws restricting its possession therefore violated a citizen's freedom to decide what is best for himself.

Mr. Smith said he would also argue that alcohol was more harmful than marijuana, and that Pennsylvania unfairly discriminated against marijuana users when it banned marijuana but not alcohol. Mr. Smith, long active in civil liberties causes, said the case would give the Court a "historic opportunity to redefine the boundaries between government control and individual liberty."

Pennsylvania's Case Stated

Arguing for the Commonwealth of Pennsylvania will be its Attorney General, Robinson M. Peters. Mr. Peters said yesterday in Harrisburg that he would argue *(Continued)*

(Continued) that marijuana was potentially dangerous and that laws prohibiting it were rational attempts to control what he called a "very serious problem of growing drug abuse and escapism."

Mr. Rodriguez, a gasoline station attendant, was convicted of marijuana possession by a trial court in Harrisburg. With the backing of the American Civil Liberties Union, he appealed to the Pennsylvania Supreme Court on the grounds that the state's marijuana laws were illegal. His appeal was rejected in April 1970 in a 6-1 decision. He has been free during his appeals to higher courts.

Mr. Rodriguez, who was born in Puerto Rico and who came to the mainland with his family at the age of 11, maintains he has never used marijuana. At his trial in Harrisburg, he said the marijuana cigarettes were given to him by youths who had driven into his station for gasoline. Later the same evening, while he was examining the dead battery of a police car that had stalled near his station, the two cigarettes, encased in a small plastic bag, fell to the street from his shirt pocket and he was arrested for possession.

Defendant Explains Position

In an interview here yesterday, Mr. Rodriguez said he had been moved to attack Pennsylvania's marijuana law in his appeal only after the trial judge who convicted him said that Rodriguez' sentence would be "an example to Rodriguez and to young people generally of the penalties for fooling around with dangerous drugs." Rodriguez said that "bad justice" was being handed down by courts throughout the United States because of such laws. He also repeated his assertion that he had never used marijuana and said he had no intention of doing so even if the laws against it were upset.

"The kids who came to the station that night put those cigarettes in my pocket and I forgot all about them," he said. "But when I was convicted it made me think how much laws like that were hurting people. So I asked my lawyer and he got me some outside help to appeal."

The New York Times, February 13, 1972

It is February 14, 1972, the day of the argument in the marijuana case. The Washington wind is blowing the remnants of a powdery snow into little swirls as you walk up the marble steps of the Supreme Court of the United States. You walk through the bronze doors that are ornately carved with scenes recounting developments in the history of law and cross the high chambered corridor leading to the courtroom. Although it is early, a crowd has already formed a line.

At 9:45 A.M., the guard unhooks the velvet-shrouded rope and the people walk slowly through the main doors of the courtroom, and around the maroon curtain that stands as a breakwater at the entrance. As you enter, a guard hands you a piece of paper:

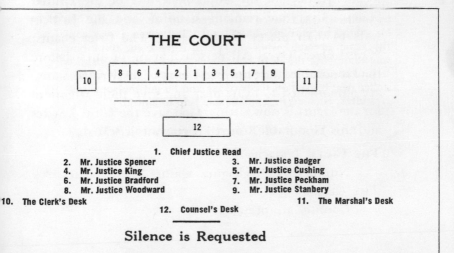

THE COURT

| 10 | | 8 | 6 | 4 | 2 | 1 | 3 | 5 | 7 | 9 | | 11 |

— — — — — — — —

| 12 |

1. Chief Justice Read
2. Mr. Justice Spencer
3. Mr. Justice Badger
4. Mr. Justice King
5. Mr. Justice Cushing
6. Mr. Justice Bradford
7. Mr. Justice Peckham
8. Mr. Justice Woodward
9. Mr. Justice Stanbery
10. The Clerk's Desk
11. The Marshal's Desk
12. Counsel's Desk

Silence is Requested

You take a seat on one of the red-cushioned wooden benches in the rear half of the courtroom. Commanding the room is the Justices' bench with its nine empty leather-backed chairs set behind a long mahogany desk raised on a dais. Directly in front are the tables for the attorneys and, behind them, the area reserved for the press and those lawyers who have been admitted to practice before the Court. The focal point of the room is the mahogany lectern from which each advocate will, in turn, attempt to persuade the Court of the correctness of his position. It stands between the two counsel tables and is directly opposite the chair of the Chief Justice. The chairs of the various Justices are different: Some are high-backed, others are not, some are tufted, while others are smooth. You look at the little piece of paper and mentally match each name with the empty chairs.

A faint buzzer sounds, then a loud knock. A hush falls over the courtroom, everyone stands, and the Crier chants: "The Honorable, the Chief Justice and the Associate Justices of the Supreme Court of the United States." Everyone remains standing and the Justices walk to their places on the bench. The Crier chants: "Oyez! Oyez! Oyez! All persons having business before the Honorable, the Supreme Court of the United States, are admonished to draw near and give their attention, for the Court is now sitting. God save the United States and this Honorable Court!" Everyone is seated.

THE CHIEF JUSTICE:

Number 65, Rodriguez against Pennsylvania.

THE CLERK:

Counsel are present.

6

PART TWO

Argument on Behalf of Peter Rodriguez

THE CHIEF JUSTICE:

Mr. Smith, you may begin.

MR. SMITH:

Mr. Chief Justice, and may it please the Court. This could be a momentous point in history. For today we seek reaffirmation of what the late Mr. Justice Brandeis has characterized as "the most comprehensive of rights and the right most valued by civilized man"—the "right to be let alone." We believe that the government cannot tell us how to live our lives—what we can read, think, eat, drink, or even smoke—without demonstrating that the clear and present danger of our actions so imperils society or endangers ourselves that the need for regulation outweighs our right to be let alone. We respectfully submit that the use of marijuana does not present such a clear and present danger and that people have a constitutionally protected right to smoke marijuana, if they so desire, in their pursuit of happiness. In a nutshell, we are asking this Court to legalize marijuana.

MR. JUSTICE BADGER:

That's a pretty big nutshell.

MR. SMITH:

Not at all, Mr. Justice Badger. The right of people to be free from government intrusion into their private affairs is a right that we submit is guaranteed by the Constitution. The government may abridge this fundamental human right to be let alone only if it demonstrates that there is a compelling interest to do so. As I will show later, society's interest in banning marijuana does not outweigh the right of people to use it if they wish.

This is an appeal from the conviction of Peter Rodriguez for possessing two marijuana cigarettes. He was sentenced to three years' imprisonment with two and one-half years of the sentence suspended.

MR. JUSTICE SPENCER:

Was he a pusher?

MR. SMITH:

No, Mr. Justice Spencer. That is what happened. On July 19, 1969, Rodriguez, who is married and the father of twin girls, was working his regular night shift at a gas station just inside the city limits of Harrisburg. At about 11:00 P.M., a green Mustang with two young couples pulled into the station. They were all laughing, and after Rodriguez sold them some gas, the driver said: "Hey, fellow —ever take grass?" My client replied that he never had, and wasn't particularly interested in trying some because he had heard that it was dangerous and, besides, it was against the law. The young man laughed and replied that marijuana "was really groovy." Before he drove off, he stuffed a little plastic food-wrap bag in Rodriguez' pocket and said: "Here, live a little." The bag contained two marijuana cigarettes. Somewhat stunned and

10

uncertain as to what he should do, Rodriguez left the bag in his shirt pocket.

MR. JUSTICE WOODWARD:

Did he know these people?

MR. SMITH:

No, Mr. Justice Woodward. He did not. They were perfect strangers. He never saw them before or afterward. Sometime later, Rodriguez went to aid a police car that had stalled near the station. As Rodriguez was bending over the engine to determine what was wrong, the little plastic bag with the marijuana cigarettes fell out of his pocket. One of the policemen saw it fall and went over to investigate. Rodriguez had retrieved the bag and was in the process of replacing it when the officer asked, almost jokingly, whether the little brown cigarettes he had seen in the bag were marijuana. Rodriguez replied: "I guess so." That was that. He was arrested, tried, and convicted for unlawfully possessing marijuana, and was sentenced to three years' imprisonment under Pennsylvania law, which provides that one who is guilty of unlawfully possessing marijuana, and is a first offender, can be fined up to two thousand dollars and can be imprisoned by "separate or solitary confinement at labor" for from two to five years. As I have already stated, Rodriguez was given three years with all but six months of the sentence suspended. His conviction and sentence have been upheld by the Supreme Court of Pennsylvania, from which this appeal is taken.

Now, we submit that the United States Constitution does not permit the commonwealth of Pennsylvania, or any state for that matter, to make criminal the private possession or the personal use of marijuana.

MR. JUSTICE WOODWARD:

Your client wasn't convicted for using marijuana, was he?

MR. SMITH:

No, Your Honor. He was convicted for merely having two marijuana cigarettes in his possession.

MR. JUSTICE WOODWARD:

Then why argue a point you don't have to?

MR. SMITH:

As I will show later on, the fact that Rodriguez did not use the marijuana or have any intention of using it is another reason why his conviction must be reversed. But I must candidly admit that in the usual case, possession and use are brigaded together, and therefore, with the Court's permission, I will examine the problem in its entirety. While I would naturally be very happy indeed if this Court were to reverse Rodriguez' conviction for any reason, if this Court were to lay down a general rule with respect to marijuana . . .

MR. JUSTICE PECKHAM:

You realize that we don't decide constitutional questions except as they may relate to specific cases?

MR. SMITH:

I do, Your Honor—but even on the facts of this case, if you reject our narrow argument, the Court will have to deal with the constitutional implications surrounding the use of marijuana. For, in all candor, I don't see how this Court will say "you can possess marijuana, but you cannot use it." That would be like saying "you can go to the beach, but don't go near the water."

MR. JUSTICE WOODWARD:

That's not so. One can possess guns—but one can't shoot people with them.

MR. JUSTICE PECKHAM:

Well, aren't you really saying that a person can possess guns for use in hunting or as display pieces, but that a person will only possess marijuana cigarettes to smoke?

MR. SMITH:

Yes, sir. Now we contend that the laws prohibiting the possession and use of marijuana are unconstitutional and that, in any event, Rodriguez did not possess marijuana with the intent to use or to sell it, and for that additional reason we submit that his conviction should be reversed.

Now, our first point is that a person's private pursuit of pleasure is protected by the Bill of Rights and that the government cannot interfere with that "pursuit of happiness" unless it can show an overriding social need that makes such interference necessary. To phrase it another way, the government must show that the individual's private actions present a clear and compelling danger either to himself or to society. We will show this Court that smoking marijuana does not present such a threat and that the reasons for which marijuana was prohibited, and the reasons why some people fight legalization today, are not supported by scientific evidence and are not valid.

THE CHIEF JUSTICE:

You are aware, are you not, that several courts, including the Supreme Court of Pennsylvania in this case, have disagreed and have held that the ban on the possession of marijuana is constitutional?

MR. SMITH:

I am, Mr. Chief Justice. But we believe that the decisions in those cases were based upon an overly narrow reading of the Constitution. We respectfully submit that the Bill of Rights—as made applicable to the states by the Fourteenth Amendment—protects the person's private pursuit of pleasure from unwarranted governmental restriction. We will demonstrate that the prohibitions on the possession or use of marijuana are not founded upon scientific or social necessity and that they are therefore unwarranted.

MR. JUSTICE SPENCER:

Isn't that a judgment for the legislature? We can't sit as a superlegislative body to decide what laws are needed and what are not.

MR. SMITH:

That certainly would be true in the ordinary case. But this Court has consistently held that fundamental human rights can be abridged only if the government can show a counterbalancing and compelling social interest. We submit that all the available scientific evidence clearly demonstrates that there is no such compelling social interest that warrants the prohibition of marijuana.

MR. JUSTICE BRADFORD:

But isn't scientific evidence better presented to the legislatures than to this Court?

MR. SMITH:

No, Your Honor. If the available evidence demonstrates that there is no compelling need for marijuana's prohibition, we submit that the prohibition is unconstitutional. Thus, in order for this Court to determine whether the prohibition is indeed supported by such a need, it must look at all the evidence. For example, in 1954, the legislatures in many of our states felt, as I am sure some of them still feel today, that segregation of the races in the public schools was both socially proper and scientifically valid. But, in that year this Court, in the landmark case of *Brown* v. *Board of Education,* reviewed the available scientific evidence and concluded not only that segregation was not supportable by scientific evidence, but also that, indeed, all the available psychological evidence demonstrated that it was harmful to the Negro children, and that their constitutional rights were being violated by the enforced separation. Similarly here, as we will show, the weight of the scientific evidence demonstrates that the ban on marijuana is not founded upon a compelling social need and that the laws prohibiting its possession and use are an unconstitutional invasion into people's private affairs.

Our second point is that marijuana is less dangerous to society than alcohol and that the government, in prohibiting the one and not the other, denies equal protection of the laws to those who take the marijuana route to pleasure and relaxation.

Third, we submit that Rodriguez' conviction for merely possessing marijuana, without any attempt to show that he intended to use it or to sell it, is an imposition of cruel and unusual punishment in violation of the Eighth Amendment to the Constitution of the United States.

MR. JUSTICE CUSHING:

On your first point, I think it is settled that the government may prohibit the possession and use of various substances by virtue of its inherent right to protect the individual, other people, and, indeed, itself. If the legislature thinks that marijuana is harmful, how can we interfere?

MR. SMITH:

This Court has the ultimate responsibility in determining whether there is in fact a compelling need for the government to tell me what I can or cannot do in the privacy of my home.

MR. JUSTICE BRADFORD:

Where in the Constitution do you find that the possession and use of marijuana is a fundamental human right that can be abridged only if there is a compelling reason to do so?

MR. SMITH:

Over a hundred years ago, in his classic essay *On Liberty,* John Stuart Mill noted that the government's exercise of its power over the individual was limited. He wrote that "the only purpose for which power can be rightfully exercised over any member of a civilized community against his will is to prevent harm to others. His own good, either

16

physical or moral, is not a sufficient warrant."
While we might not go so far as Mill—for example, we will concede that the government can constitutionally ban the use or even the possession of
something that physically harms the user—we submit that the guarantees found in the Bill of Rights
and in the Fourteenth Amendment, which forbids
any state from depriving any person of life, liberty,
or property without due process of law, preserve
to the individual a right to privacy—privacy of
thought and action. This is made clear by several
recent decisions of this Court.

In 1965, this Court, in the case of *Griswold* v.
Connecticut, recognized that the individual is protected by a constitutional wall of privacy and that
the government cannot breach that wall without
showing a compelling need to do so. The *Griswold*
case concerned the constitutionality of a Connecticut statute that prohibited anyone from using or
prescribing the use of contraceptives. The exec-
utive director and the medical director of the
Connecticut Planned Parenthood League were
convicted for violating that law because they ad-
vised married couples in the use of contraceptives.
This Court reversed their convictions and held that
the Connecticut law violated the right of marital
privacy. This was an important step—for, as the
dissenters pointed out, the Constitution does not
specifically guarantee a right of marital privacy.
But the Court recognized that the specific guarantees in the Bill of Rights—for example, the First
Amendment's guarantee of free speech and the

17

right of free association, the Third and Fourth Amendments' protection of the sanctity of the home by prohibiting the peacetime quartering of soldiers in any house and unreasonable searches and seizures—create zones of privacy into which the government cannot penetrate unless there are very exceptional circumstances where such penetration is absolutely necessary to preserve some overriding social interest. This Court decided that the use of contraceptives, by married persons at least, was within the wall of privacy that could not be breached by Connecticut's desire to prevent promiscuity within its borders.

THE CHIEF JUSTICE:

Do you contend that the use of marijuana is also protected by a wall of privacy?

MR. SMITH:

We do, Mr. Chief Justice. I would say that everything a person may wish to do in the privacy of his home is protected by that wall. The real question is whether the government has a compelling interest in forbidding the activity. If it does, then that wall of privacy will offer no protection. For example, I would not argue that a father should have, as he had in ancient Rome, absolute power over his children so that he could, for instance, abuse his child or sell him into slavery, even though such a "right" ostensibly would be protected not only by the privacy of the home but also by the privacy of the family. Society's interest in protecting children is too great and would prevail. Thus, compulsory education is constitutional. There is a compelling social need to have educated citizens, and this social interest overrides the right of an individual parent to bring up his children as he wishes. But where the state cannot demonstrate a compelling social need to regulate the private affairs of its citizens, it cannot constitutionally do so. Thus, as this Court held in *Meyer* v. *Nebraska* in 1923, fundamental human rights—what I like to call the wall of privacy—prevented the state of Nebraska from forbidding children below a certain age from learning German. This Court noted that the state's interest in seeing to it that everyone knew English was not a sufficient reason to deny parents their fundamental right to have their children know a foreign language if they so wished, as long as the children were also taught English.

MR. JUSTICE CUSHING:

Then, as you see it, all human activity is protected from government regulation by this so-called wall of privacy and only a compelling governmental or societal interest will permit the government to regulate or forbid the activity?

MR. SMITH:

Precisely. In most instances, however, we don't recognize that the wall of privacy exists because the need for governmental regulation is so clear. Thus, no one would seriously contend that a driver has the "right to be let alone" and thus can't be forced to obey traffic rules. His activity directly affects others and thus needs to be regulated. However, where an individual's actions have no direct or indirect effect on others, or upon society as a whole, then this right to be let alone—this right of privacy —becomes paramount. A recent decision of this Court makes this abundantly clear.

In *Stanley* v. *Georgia,* a man was convicted for violating a Georgia law that made the knowing possession of obscene material punishable by imprisonment for from one to five years. Now, this Court has held that while the First Amendment protects the right to disseminate ideas, it does not protect the dissemination of obscenity. In most cases, therefore, the question is whether a given book or a given film is obscene. If it is obscene, it is not protected by the First Amendment, and selling it or transporting it through the mails can be prohibited. But Stanley was not convicted for selling obscene material. He was convicted for merely possessing, and ostensibly viewing, several reels of pornographic film in his apartment. This Court assumed that the film was obscene and was therefore not protected by the First Amendment as such. But Stanley's right to look at it in his home was nevertheless protected by the Constitution. This Court, while noting that the person who traffics in obscenity clearly affects society and that therefore society has a valid interest in regulating his activity, also concluded that society's interest in preventing people from reading dirty books or looking at pornographic movies was less clear. It would have to be balanced against the right of the person "to be let alone." As Mr. Justice Marshall said in writing for the Court, ". . . fundamental is the right to be free, except in very limited circumstances, from unwarranted governmental intrusions into one's privacy." Thus, if Stanley's private possession of obscenity did not substantially affect other individuals or society, he would be protected by the wall of privacy. Inquiry was therefore made as to whether those "limited circumstances" were present, that is, whether there was a compelling social need or governmental interest that would permit the state of Georgia to say to Stanley, "You cannot own dirty movies and you cannot watch them." This Court decided that there was not.

First, it rejected Georgia's assertion that it had the constitutional power to protect Stanley's mind from obscenity, and it held that the morality of Stanley's thoughts was his own business. Second, the Court rejected Georgia's argument that it could prohibit the private possession and viewing of pornographic movies because exposure to obscenity may lead to deviant sexual behavior or crimes of sexual violence. The Court noted that there was little scientific basis for this argument and that, in any event, criminal behavior could be prevented by the usual methods of education and punishment. In short, the Court noted that Georgia could "no more prohibit mere possession of obscene matter on the ground that it may lead to antisocial conduct than it may prohibit possession of chemistry books on the ground that they may lead to the manufacture of homemade spirits."

Stanley's possession of obscenity was thus protected by the Constitution's wall of privacy; more-

over, as Mr. Justice Marshall then wrote for the
Court, because there was no compelling reason for
the government to interfere into his private affairs,
Stanley had the unfettered "right to satisfy his intellectual and emotional needs in the privacy of
his own home." We respectfully submit that the
same reasoning applies to this case and that because there is no compelling reason that permits
the government to invade the sanctuary of privacy
and prohibit the private possession and personal
use of marijuana, the person who seeks to use
marijuana to satisfy his intellectual, emotional, and
physical needs has the unfettered right to do so.

MR. JUSTICE CUSHING:
Assuming that we agree with your formulation of
the constitutional right of privacy, and assuming
that we agree that its scope is broad enough to
cover the private use of marijuana, doesn't the
government have a sufficiently strong reason to
prohibit even the private possession and use of
marijuana? You said earlier that you disagree with
John Stuart Mill at least to the extent that you
believe government can prevent people from harm-
ing themselves. Why isn't this a sufficient reason
to forbid people from using marijuana?

MR. SMITH:
Your Honor, there is no scientific evidence that
marijuana is either dangerous to society or harmful
to the user.

MR. JUSTICE WOODWARD:
Is there any evidence that it is not harmful?

MR. SMITH:
Yes, Your Honor, there is.

MR. JUSTICE WOODWARD:

Then why has it been banned not only in this country but also in others as well? Isn't that some indication that it is harmful?

MR. SMITH:

Normally, I would say yes. But the history of marijuana and its prohibition makes this a special case. Let us first define our terms. What is marijuana? Marijuana is made by taking the topmost leaves, flowers, and stems of the female hemp or *Cannabis* plant and drying them and is only one of the intoxicating products of that plant. Its intoxicating quality comes from a sticky resinous material that is secreted by the female plant. Hashish, by the way, is the dried form of the pure hemp resin and is many times stronger than marijuana. Hemp itself has been around for many thousands of years, its first recorded use being over two thousand years before Christ, when the Chinese emperor Shen Nung listed it in his herbal compendium. The hemp plant is widely used in India, where many regard it as holy. The Atharva-Veda describes it as a sacred grass, and the guardian angel of mankind is supposed to reside in its leaves. Hindus refer to it as the "heavenly guide" or the "poor man's heaven" because of its intoxicating qualities. While marijuana is usually smoked in this country in the form of cigarettes, people in India dry the leaves, flowers, and stems to form what they call bhang, and they make a very popular beverage by brewing this together with sugar, pepper, and other spices. Bhang is also used extensively in India as an ingredient in various foods, especially candy and cakes.

Bhang ice cream is also very popular. By compressing and curing the leaves and flowers, the Indians produce a substance that they call ganja, which is more powerful than bhang but less potent than hashish. Bhang is the weakest hemp product and is equivalent in potency to the marijuana that is commonly smoked in this country.

In the past, hemp was also widely used for its fiber in the manufacture of twine and textiles. In fact, in the early history of this country, hemp was a very valuable cash crop and was cultivated extensively. Even George Washington grew hemp. The invention of the cotton gin and the steam engine, however, reduced its importance as a source of fiber, and hemp is now cultivated around the world mainly for its intoxicating properties.

History is replete with references to its use as an intoxicant—for example, not only was it widely used for this purpose in Asia but also in the fifth century B.C. Herodotus noted how the Scythians used to throw hemp on hot ashes and rocks and breathe in the resulting fumes. On this continent, however, its ability to produce euphoria was probably first discovered by the Indians living in Mexico. The word "marijuana" is thought to come from the Spanish corruption of the Portuguese word "mariguano," which means "intoxicated."

Now, in answer to Your Honor's question, the intoxicating products of the hemp or *Cannabis* plant have been banned in many countries because there has been little distinction between these products, which vary in potency, and also because there

24

has been much misinformation. For example, hash-ish, which as I've noted is the pure resin of the hemp plant, is some six times as potent as mari-juana, and marijuana has been blamed for much of what is properly attributable to an overindul-gence in hashish. Even hashish may have been falsely accused, however. For example, from the end of the eleventh to the thirteenth century, a sect headed by a series of leaders known as the "Old Man of the Mountains" spread terror throughout Persia and Syria. This sect, which was sort of an early-day version of Murder Incorporated, sought to assassinate all of its political and religious ene-mies. Legend has it that members took hashish to induce ecstatic visions of paradise before they set out on their dangerous missions. They thus became known as "Hashishin," or hashish eaters, from which we get our word "assassin."

Some thirty years after the extirpation of the sect, however, Marco Polo visited the regions where it had flourished, and he tells a slightly different story. He reported that youthful converts to the sect would be drugged with opium, not hashish, and rendered unconscious. They were then placed in a sumptuous garden and regained consciousness to find themselves surrounded by beautiful women who satisfied their every desire. After several days of orgiastic pleasure, they were drugged again and removed from the garden. When they awoke, they were told that they had been in paradise, to which they would return if they were killed in the service of the Old Man of the Mountains. After this experience, they enthusiastically went off to commit murder for their leader.

Although Marco Polo reported that opium was used and not hashish, this early association of hashish with murder has persisted to modern times. For example, because it was widely believed in India that the use of the hemp or cannabis drugs causes insanity and violent criminal behavior, a study of the extent and nature of cannabis use in that country was undertaken in the 1890s. In 1894, the Indian Hemp Drugs Commission, after an extensive investigation, reported that moderate use of cannabis produces no ill effects at all and even excessive use does not lead to the commission of violent crimes. Similarly, marijuana has been falsely blamed in this country for a myriad of ills, and error has been compounded with error, with the result that today every state has harsh and cruel penalties for the possession or sale of marijuana.

Although the various products of the *Cannabis* plant have been used throughout the world for centuries, marijuana only came into widespread use here early in this century, when it was introduced by Mexican laborers and American seamen returning from the Mexican ports. By the 1920s and the 1930s the use had become widespread among the lower social classes. As more and more people began to use marijuana, some officials, having lost the prohibition fight with alcohol, decided that something should be done to stop the people from using this new intoxicant. So in the 1930s the Treasury Department's Bureau of Narcotics started an intensive campaign to warn the public of the so-called dangers of marijuana. It was called "the killer weed," and there were stories of how people who smoked marijuana would go insane and how horrible murders and sexual crimes were committed by so-called marijuana fiends. An example of the wild and unsubstantiated nature of the charges can be seen in this brief extract from a 1937 report by a committee of the United States Senate on a bill to control marijuana:

Under the influence of this drug, the will is destroyed and all power of directing and controlling thought is lost. Inhibitions are released. As a result of these effects, many violent crimes have been and are being committed by persons under the influence of this drug. Not only is marijuana used by hardened criminals to steel them to commit violent crimes, but it is also being placed in the hands of high school children in the form of marijuana cigarettes by unscrupulous peddlers. Its continued use results many times in impotency and insanity.

This report to Congress was not based on hard evidence. Rather, the only so-called support was isolated newspaper accounts and hearsay stories. For example, one of the stories used to support the banning of marijuana concerned a young Floridian; let me quote this story, as recounted in a typical scare pamphlet published in 1939:

Ralph Adam Fine

Victor Licata, age 19, sat sobbing. He was in jail in Tampa, Florida, his hometown; and, although he had been there half a day, his parents had not been to see him. He wondered why they had forgotten or were neglecting him. This was why he was crying. He didn't know that his mother and father were dead; that his whole family, except a brother away at the University, had been killed. He knew they were alive the day before; he had been with them then. Now, he didn't know they were dead, and what is more, he didn't know that he was the one who had killed them! He didn't remember that in the middle of the night he had arisen, taken an axe, and hacked his mother, father, two brothers and sister to pieces while they slept. He didn't know any of this; but the police did—all of it. What the police did not know was why he had killed his family. As they questioned him, he was bewildered, confused, and even surprised that his folks were dead, and astounded when they told him that he had killed them. After the police had told the boy why he was in jail, he told them what he could remember of what happened prior to his killing five members of his family. It was an incoherent story. He had spent most of the night, so he said, trying to prevent someone from cutting off his arms and legs. Under patient questioning, the story was eventually pieced together. Victor had smoked some marijuana cigarettes

28

that afternoon. After going to bed that night, he suddenly thought, as nightmarish hallucinations raced through his mind, that his mother and father were plotting to cut off his arms and legs as soon as they got up in the morning. This horrible obsession transfixed itself in his mind; and so real was this imagined threat to him that he decided that the only thing to do was to kill them first, while they slept.

Yes, it's true—on October 17, 1933, one Victor Licata axed his father, mother, sister, and two brothers to death. It seems, however, that a year before, the police had filed a lunacy petition seeking to have Licata committed. The petition was withdrawn because his parents felt that they could give him better treatment at home. After he was arrested, Licata was examined and found to be criminally insane. Unable to stand trial, he was committed to the Florida State Mental Hospital, where his behavior continued to be "overtly psychotic" until he hanged himself on December 4, 1950. Licata was not the quiet lad plunged into fits of frenzied killings by marijuana—he was sick, evidently hopelessly sick. Not only was there no evidence that marijuana caused his derangement but also the mental hospital records do not mention that Licata even used the drug. Yet this was the type of flimsy foundation upon which the case against marijuana was built and as a result of the hysteria and misinformation, Congress passed the

Marijuana Tax Act of 1937 and every state has out-lawed marijuana.

MR. JUSTICE WOODWARD:

You say "misinformation." Wasn't there testimony about criminal activity in New Orleans being associated with the use of marijuana?

MR. SMITH:

You're correct, Mr. Justice Woodward. There was testimony that 125 of the 450 men who committed major crimes in New Orleans in 1930 smoked marijuana. But this figure, if the Court please, is grossly misleading. First, it is sheer guilt by association; a causal relationship was implied but not shown. It would be just as correct to say that all the men drank water and that therefore water causes criminal activity. Second, marijuana was used in New Orleans in the twenties and thirties by essentially the lower social classes and the criminal element, so that naturally any type of dragnet applied to these groups would yield a high percentage of marijuana smokers. It's just that the people who used marijuana were also the social and economic outcasts, the people who committed crimes. Third, the figure may not even be accurate. There is no reliable method of revealing the presence of marijuana in a person's body, so you have to take the word of the criminal that he was indeed a marijuana user.

MR. JUSTICE WOODWARD:

Why would he say that he was taking marijuana if he was not? Why should he admit to an additional crime?

Mary Jane versus Pennsylvania

MR. SMITH:

The criminal would say he was acting under the influence of marijuana in the hope of avoiding responsibility for his crime. In 1930, the maximum penalty for possession of marijuana in Louisiana was six months.

Now, as I've noted, a morass of misleading and inaccurate information stampeded the Congress and the states to outlaw marijuana. Laws were passed forbidding the possession of marijuana, and violators are subject to outrageously long prison terms. For example, in the late 1960s a Virginia youth was sentenced to twenty years for possessing 6½ pounds of marijuana that he had purchased for some friends. Fortunately, the governor saw fit to pardon him. In any event, the thirties saw frantic activity, and everyone jumped on the bandwagon, recounting the supposed horrors of marijuana. Everyone, that is, except Fiorello LaGuardia, who was then the mayor of New York City. He was concerned over reports that marijuana was being used by many New York City residents, including high school students, and that it caused widespread criminal conduct. But his concern was tempered by what he remembered. When he was a congressman, he had reviewed a report by the Army concerning the use of marijuana by soldiers stationed in Panama. The report had emphasized that marijuana was relatively harmless. LaGuardia set out to resolve this seeming contradiction. He appointed a panel of distinguished doctors and criminologists to study the effect of marijuana on the population

31

of New York City. This was the first attempt at
a scientific study of marijuana in this country, and
its results were astounding. The report, issued by
the panel in 1944, confirmed what the Army had
discovered in its previous investigations in 1925
and 1933, when the Army had concluded that
marijuana was not addictive and that it had no
"appreciably deleterious influence on the individuals using it."

The LaGuardia committee study was in two
parts. In the first, the police commissioner assigned
special undercover agents to infiltrate the society
of marijuana users and to live among them. They
found approximately five hundred commercial
marijuana parlors—or "tea pads," as they were
called—scattered throughout Manhattan but concentrated in the Harlem area. These tea pads were,
for the most part, comfortably decorated rooms
where the smokers relaxed, listened to music, or
just talked. In a sense, they were congenial social
clubs. The investigators reported that the patrons
were friendly and no one got boisterous or rowdy.
The users themselves indicated that they did not
think marijuana was harmful. They smoked it
openly, unlike the narcotic drug addict, who would
take his fix in secret. They also found that marijuana was not habit-forming and that the marijuana user did not even experience frustration
when he was unable to get his normal supply of
cigarettes. They reported that marijuana made
people hungry and that, while users were smoking
it, they did not drink liquor. They further re-

ported that marijuana seemed to give the smokers a feeling of adequacy and self-confidence which they otherwise lacked. Additionally, the investigators found no evidence to support the widely-held belief that marijuana smokers "graduated" to heroin or the other hard drugs. Nor did they notice any apparent mental or physical deterioration among habitual marijuana users.

Aside from these observations in the field, the LaGuardia committee also conducted controlled experiments on a group of volunteers who were drawn from the various New York City prisons. Marijuana was administered to the subjects in pill form, and their reactions were compared with the reactions of others who had received placebos. One experiment was conducted under tea pad conditions and the subjects were given cigarettes rather than pills. The results of these controlled experiments confirmed what the undercover agents had observed in the field: the subjects, after taking marijuana, generally had lowered inhibitions and talked freely; they gained more self-confidence and generally became less aggressive and belligerent.

MR. JUSTICE BRADFORD:
Didn't the investigators also observe what they termed psychotic reactions among some of the subjects?

MR. SMITH:
They did, Mr. Justice Bradford. Three of the patients who were given large doses of marijuana extract in pill form did suffer from temporary psychoses—but they were all psychotic personalities

drawn from a prison population. One of the three did not develop his psychosis until two weeks after the experiment had been completed and he was returned to prison. He had hoped to be allowed to stay at the hospital, and the LaGuardia committee felt that his reaction could properly be traced to prison psychosis unrelated to marijuana. Six other subjects had minor adverse reactions with the pills that quickly went away. It was concluded that "the few psychotic episodes that occurred are exactly what we would expect in the whole group without considering the administration and effects of excessive doses of marijuana" and that while marijuana may release psychoses in persons already suffering from some sort of psychological illness, it will not alter a person's basic psychological structure.

MR. JUSTICE SPENCER:

You mean to say that if a person is predisposed to mental illness, marijuana might trigger it?

MR. SMITH:

In those people who are so predisposed, marijuana might produce hallucinations and disorientation, but it will not cause permanent mental injury.

MR. JUSTICE SPENCER:

It seems to me that you are saying the marijuana could release the Mr. Hydes which are lurking in all of us.

MR. SMITH:

No, not at all, Your Honor. Marijuana does not alter the individual's basic personality. The LaGuardia committee specifically found that marijuana will not cause mental illness.

34

Mary Jane versus Pennsylvania

MR. JUSTICE SPENCER:

Did LaGuardia recommend legalizing it?

MR. SMITH:

No, he did not, Your Honor. He felt that there was insufficient knowledge at the time to recommend legalizing it. But almost thirty years have passed, and despite a recent spate of research activity and widespread use of marijuana in this country, there is absolutely no serious evidence that marijuana is either harmful to the user or dangerous to society. This being the case, there are insufficient grounds to warrant governmental interference into the private affairs of its citizens. The LaGuardia committee study exposed many of the myths about marijuana, and more recent research has reaffirmed its conclusions.

Now, many people who oppose legalization of marijuana do so for various reasons. First, they say that it is harmful to the individual user. Second, they say that marijuana users are dangerous to society because marijuana induces people to commit crimes and to engage in other antisocial activity. Third, they say that even if marijuana is not harmful in and of itself and even if it doesn't cause criminal activity, its use leads to heroin addiction. All of these premises, I maintain, are invalid.

First of all, marijuana does not harm the individual user. The person who smokes a marijuana cigarette will experience few physical effects. His eyes will redden and he may feel a slight burning sensation in his throat. If he is particularly nervous, he may get nauseated. The mental effects of

35

marijuana will come on within fifteen to thirty
minutes and will usually last a few hours. At first,
the smoker will feel a sense of excitement or ten-
sion, followed by a pervasive feeling of joyousness
during which he is more aware of his surroundings.
Colors, tastes, and sounds are more intense and
seem more meaningful. And often, a person's
thoughts will tend toward the spiritual. There
will also be a distortion of perception as to time
and distance. The smoker becomes tranquil and
will peacefully enjoy his environment. As opposed
to alcohol, marijuana rarely leaves a hangover.
Increased dosages may make the user initially feel
anxious, but he will soon enter the passive or
euphoric stage. Now it is clear, and everyone agrees,
that marijuana is not habit-forming.

MR. JUSTICE PECKHAM:

Do you mean habit-forming or physically addictive?

MR. SMITH:

I am sorry, Your Honor, I mean physically addictive. All of the scientific reports and all of the
studies have shown that marijuana, unlike the
opiates, is not physically addictive. Marijuana does
not produce a physical dependence requiring con-
stant use to prevent painful withdrawal symptoms.
It also does not produce tolerance; that is, more
of the drug is not needed each time to produce the
desired results.

MR. JUSTICE PECKHAM:

But marijuana is habit-forming, is that not right?

MR. SMITH:

It can be said that it is habit-forming only in the

sense that anything which is pleasurable can be habit-forming. Candy, gum, or even television viewing or sex can be habit-forming. But the studies have shown, for example, that it is easier to quit smoking marijuana than it is to give up tobacco. In the words of the report of the President's Commission on Law Enforcement and the Administration of Justice, published in 1967, "physical dependence does not develop."

MR. JUSTICE WOODWARD:

Does your description reflect what happens to every marijuana smoker? I remember reading that marijuana use can induce depression or panic, and I think you mentioned that it might make some people nauseated.

MR. SMITH:

Let me clarify that, Mr. Justice Woodward. Marijuana smoking, like tobacco smoking, or even tying one's shoes, has to be learned. First, unless the marijuana cigarette is inhaled properly, it will produce no effects at all. In fact, Dr. Stanley F. Yolles, a former director of the National Institute of Mental Health, reported that 50 percent of the people who first try marijuana do not get any result at all. The marijuana cigarette has to be inhaled deeply, and the smoke has to be kept in the lungs for ten to twenty seconds in order for the smoker to feel its effects. Most marijuana smokers have to learn how to get high on marijuana. In a recent scientific experiment, conducted by doctors at the Boston University School of Medicine, it was shown that all but one of the subjects who had

37

never before smoked marijuana failed to get high, even though they were given very large doses. Interestingly enough, the one subject who had never tried marijuana before and who did feel some reaction had, prior to the experiment, expressed a desire to get high.

Second, a first-time experience with marijuana, as with almost anything else, can be unsettling. Just as the youngster who tries his first tobacco cigarette or cigar will most likely get ill, the same thing may happen to the person who first smokes marijuana. But, and this is important, once a person becomes experienced with marijuana, he knows how to smoke it and how to get high. He knows how to control it. In short, like drinking alcohol or smoking tobacco cigarettes, smoking marijuana has to be learned, but—and here is where marijuana is quite unlike liquor—marijuana smokers report that they are able to use less of the substance to reach the same level of intoxication once they have had experience with it.

Third, there is danger in overemphasizing the words in clinical descriptions. Sometimes clinical descriptions—"panic," "disorientation," and the like—can make reactions sound pretty bad indeed. But the actual experience is not nearly so terrible. I once heard a certain activity clinically described this way: It produces heightened pulse rate, facial flushing, sweating, marked adrenal activity. Furthermore, there is frequent loss of breath, and, occasionally, feelings of dizziness and nausea ensue. Death has resulted in some instances.

Sounds pretty terrible, doesn't it, but I don't think anyone would advocate turning all the tennis courts into parking lots.

To give another example, at the turn of the century, the Regius Professor of Physics at Cambridge, England, described coffee drinkers in the following manner: "The sufferer is tremulous and loses his self-command; he is subject to fits of agitation and depression. He has a haggard appearance and as with other such agents, a renewed dose of the poison gives temporary relief, but at the cost of future misery." There are some pretty frightening clinical descriptions floating around about marijuana also, and I am sure my opponent will refer to some of them, but inquiry has to go deeper than that. Neither marijuana nor tennis nor coffee would be as popular as they are if they were as dangerous as some clinical descriptions might indicate.

THE CHIEF JUSTICE:

Is marijuana physically harmful?

MR. SMITH:

No, Your Honor. Unlike alcohol, which is physically dangerous and can lead to death, marijuana is not dangerous. An associate medical examiner in New York City reports that in his extensive autopsy experience with hundreds of marijuana users he was unable to find any evidence of physical deterioration caused by marijuana. Furthermore, he reported, and the President's Commission on Law Enforcement and the Administration of Justice found as well, that no deaths have been attributable to marijuana use. Both the LaGuardia committee report and the extensive study conducted in the 1890s by the Indian Hemp Drugs Commission indicate that the long-term consumption of moderate doses of marijuana is not harmful.

MR. JUSTICE BRADFORD:

I note you said moderate. What about excessive dosages?

MR. SMITH:

Anything taken in excess can be harmful. I am sure that if you swallowed enough marijuana you could be severely harmed. However, a 1946 study of 310 men in the Army who had used marijuana on the average for seven years revealed no mental or physical deterioration.

MR. JUSTICE STANBERY:

Didn't the American Medical Association report that repeated use of marijuana causes chronic low blood sugar?

MR. SMITH:

This has not been proven. In fact, the controlled experiments, which I referred to earlier, conducted by a group of physicians at the Boston University School of Medicine indicate that marijuana will not cause chronic low blood sugar. Let me describe this experiment, as I will be referring to its results in some detail later on. In 1968, Drs. Norman Zinberg and Andrew Weil, feeling that not enough was known about the effects and alleged dangers of marijuana, conducted controlled experiments with a group of carefully selected subjects. After having reviewed the available reports, they concluded that the earlier studies had not screened out a number of variables, which tended to weaken their validity. For example, the LaGuardia committee report was in part based on experiments conducted on volunteers selected from a prison population who were given marijuana extract pills as well as cigarettes. In order to test only the effects of marijuana when it is smoked, Drs. Zinberg and Weil chose nine tobacco smokers who had never tried marijuana and eight chronic marijuana users who were carefully selected and psychologically screened. Since there is strong evidence that indicates that the environment can affect the way people react to marijuana, the subjects were placed in a neutral setting. The researchers taught the subjects who had never tried marijuana how to smoke a marijuana cigarette and how to keep the smoke in the lungs for a predetermined length of time. As a control, the subjects were also given dummy marijuana cigarettes prepared from stalks of the male plant. It will be remembered that only the female plant has the sticky resin that gives marijuana its intoxicating qualities. Both groups of subjects were, as I have just noted, placed in a neutral environment, and they were observed while smoking. Additionally, tests were administered to determine the effect of marijuana on both physical coordination and mental acuity. The results of these experiments support our view that marijuana cannot constitutionally be prohibited.

The physical effects of marijuana were slight. First, as I have already stated, the smoking of marijuana did not lower the blood sugar, as had previously been thought. Second, the heart rate of both the subjects who were new to marijuana and those who were chronic users increased, but the heart rate of the chronic users was increased to a greater extent. There were no observable changes in the rate of breathing or in the size of the pupils. This latter finding, by the way, indicates that the increased pupil size of marijuana smokers may result from the darkened surroundings in which marijuana is usually smoked and not from any inherent property of the drug. The eyes themselves were reddened slightly because of the dilation of the blood vessels. The researchers discovered that marijuana mainly affects the brain by acting upon the higher centers of thought, memory, and perception. There was little or no influence on the low centers that control the mechanical aspects of speech and coordination. Thus, the person who is intoxicated on marijuana will not have the staggering gait or the slurred speech of one who is intoxicated on alcohol. While the performance of simple intellectual tasks was impaired when the subjects were under the influence of marijuana, the investigators found that the chronic marijuana smokers—who were able to control their actions while under its influence—performed better than did the subjects who had never smoked marijuana before. One interesting aspect of the experiment, which I alluded to earlier, was that while all of the chronic marijuana smokers could tell when they were high, as objectively measured by their pulse rate, all but one of the subjects who had never smoked marijuana before could not, even though these subjects had smoked a sufficient quantity of marijuana to get high and their pulse rate indicated that they were indeed under its influence. As I mentioned before, the one who reported that he felt intoxicated had indicated, prior to the experiment, that he wanted to get high. This, by the way, may indicate that the effects of the drug are very subjective. The experimenters concluded that marijuana does not, in and of itself, adversely affect people's mental or physical well-being.

MR. JUSTICE KING:

Didn't you say, though, that marijuana impaired the functioning of the higher centers of the brain, in such areas as perception and thinking?

MR. SMITH:

There are limited sensory distortions, Your Honor, but none beyond what you might get, let's say, from drinking liquor. Significantly, in light of all the scare material which has been disseminated by the Bureau of Narcotics and others, marijuana did not turn the subjects into madmen or sex fiends. In fact, the experimenters reported that the subjects remained calm and relaxed throughout the experiment and retained full awareness of their surroundings.

Other studies have shown that people under the influence of marijuana have their normal functioning only slightly impaired. Indeed, one marijuana researcher gave the substance to a poker player who had never before smoked marijuana. Although he was under its influence, his mental acuity was not impaired and he was able to hold his own in a game against expert players. Additionally, not only is marijuana used by a large percentage of the college student population without any adverse effects, but a study conducted at Princeton University revealed that regular marijuana smokers were in the top of their class and were functioning well above average. There is ample support for the conclusion of Drs. Zinberg and Weil that, on the basis of their review of the relevant literature as well as their own experiment, marijuana is a relatively mild and harmless intoxicant.

THE CHIEF JUSTICE:

But there have been adverse psychological reactions to marijuana. The LaGuardia committee found several, did it not?

MR. SMITH:

Not really, Mr. Chief Justice. The only adverse psychological reactions they observed occurred when they gave large doses of marijuana extract to subjects who had a history of severe psychological problems predating the use of the drug. As I noted earlier, the LaGuardia committee found that episodes of psychotic behavior were to be expected in such a group even without the administration of any drug. It is significant that in their extensive field study of actual marijuana smokers in the community, the LaGuardia committee investigators were unable to discover any evidence that marijuana adversely affected the mental stability of the user. This finding was borne out by a recent study conducted at the Bellevue Hospital Center in New York. Out of 112 persons admitted to the hospital who were using various drugs, 8 were marijuana users. All 8 had histories of psychological problems that predated their use of marijuana.

Marijuana just doesn't adversely affect normal people, and even its effect on abnormal people is purely conjectural. As Dr. Zinberg has noted, true psychotic reactions are rare among marijuana users; in fact, he calls them "psychiatric curiosities." This is important, because there has been much said concerning marijuana's alleged tendency to impair the mental health of users.

Marijuana has been used in this country in increasing quantities since the turn of the century. It has been estimated that some twelve to twenty million or so Americans have tried it at least once in their lives. Use on college campuses has hit an all-time high. Many colleges are reporting that over 50 percent of their students have tried marijuana. For example, in 1969, out of almost five hundred students at the Columbia University School of Law who responded to a questionnaire on marijuana, 69 percent said that they had smoked marijuana at least once. Twenty percent indicated that they smoked marijuana at least once a week, with an additional 30 percent smoking marijuana at least once a month. Marijuana smoking has become so widespread, Dr. Zinberg reported, that in certain age groups, people who do not use marijuana are unusual from a psychological point of view. Additionally, and ironically, prosecutors are reporting that they have a tough time in selecting juries in marijuana cases because so many people have tried it at least once.

In light of its widespread and increasing use, the fact that there has been no evidence that marijuana produces mental injury is highly significant. LSD and other hallucinogenic drugs were in use for short periods of time before their real dangers became evident. Marijuana has been used for some five thousand years, and there is still no evidence that it is dangerous. The isolated instances of psychotic behavior seen in persons who already have had extensive histories of mental illness do not change this one iota. The plain and clear fact of the matter is that no one has been able to show that marijuana induces psychoses in normal people. This is to be contrasted with the fact that 20 percent of all people in state mental hospitals are there because of problems created by alcohol.

MR. JUSTICE PECKHAM:

Wasn't there evidence that there have been some cases of mental and physical deterioration caused by use of the drug in India?

MR. SMITH:

There have been reports from India, for example, that some disturbances do develop after heavy long-term use. But even in India—as that country's 1894 Hemp Drugs Commission reported—moderate long-term use does not produce harmful effects. What adverse effects were reported are attributable to several factors. As Dr. Zinberg explained, most of the cannabis drugs that are used in India are far more potent than the marijuana that is smoked here. As I noted earlier, hashish is six times as potent as marijuana. Furthermore, the environment in which the substance is used in India is different —and there are other variables, such as malnutrition and the widespread prevalence of disease. Dr. Zinberg stated that observations based on the Indian experience "simply have no relevance to the situation in our country."

MR. JUSTICE PECKHAM:
Isn't that a bit cavalier?

MR. SMITH:
I don't think so. In 1968, a report by the British Advisory Committee on Drug Dependence also noted that there have been no reliable reports of such ill effects in the Western world. Surely, if the disturbances had been seen in India, where medical care is far from adequate, and if marijuana could produce similar disturbances here, then some examples would have turned up, especially on college campuses, where there is rampant use, and opportunity for observation is greater than elsewhere. The fact that mental disturbances traceable to marijuana have not turned up, as compared with disturbances traceable to drugs such as LSD, is a very strong indication that there is simply no such relationship. All of the available evidence clearly indicates that marijuana is a mild intoxicant that produces a mild euphoria and relaxes the smoker. Its effect is very similar to that of liquor except that, unlike alcohol, marijuana does not harm the body and leaves no hangover.

THE CHIEF JUSTICE:

Is there a danger that if restrictions on marijuana use are relaxed, more potent varieties of the drug will also be used?

MR. SMITH:

Not necessarily. Of course, marijuana cigarettes do vary in potency, but as one doctor in the field has stated, if the American smoker of marijuana inadvertently uses or smokes a more potent cigarette, he is likely to experience nothing more alarming than going to sleep and waking up hungry. Furthermore, it has been demonstrated that marijuana users know almost instinctively how much of the substance they need to make them feel relaxed and comfortably high. Once that point is reached, they will stop smoking it. Thus, one day it might take two marijuana cigarettes to accomplish the desired results, while the next day the marijuana may be more potent and only one cigarette will be smoked. That is one reason why the experiments where marijuana is given in pill form are invalid. The marijuana user's ability to self-regulate his dose is bypassed.

But all we ask here is that marijuana be legalized and that Rodriguez' conviction for merely possessing two marijuana cigarettes be overturned. Once legalized, however, marijuana, like alcohol, can be regulated and its potency can be standardized. If there is evidence, for example, that hashish is dangerous, it can still be banned. But we submit that marijuana is not dangerous and that, there being no compelling reason for its prohibition, the government cannot constitutionally impose criminal penalties for its possession and use.

MR. JUSTICE BRADFORD:

You say that if marijuana is legalized, the other harmful drugs can still be banned. I assume that this is consistent with your theory of the Bill of Rights and the Fourteenth Amendment?

MR. SMITH:

Yes, Your Honor. What I like to call the Constitution's wall of privacy protects people only from unwarranted government interference in the conduct of their own affairs. If a substance is harmful or dangerous, then the government would have the constitutional power to make its possession unlawful. But where a substance is not demonstrably harmful, beyond mere speculation, then the government cannot intrude upon a person's freedom to act as he pleases.

MR. JUSTICE BRADFORD:

Fine, but won't legalization of marijuana merely shift the allure of illegality—which is now concentrated on marijuana—to other more harmful drugs?

MR. SMITH:

I don't think so, Your Honor. Of course, there are always people who will try anything. Skydiving, for example, is a very popular sport. In 1968, over forty youngsters died trying to inhale the spray from aerosol cans. There was also a report that at a folk-rock festival in Monterey, California, it was rumored that THC, which is thought to be the chemical that gives marijuana its intoxicating properties, was going to be distributed free. Sure enough, shortly thereafter, a truck circled the area, and thousands of capsules were tossed to eagerly awaiting hands. The young flower children gobbled up the capsules, threw up, and passed out. The capsules contained not THC but PCT, a powerful animal anesthetic. Some people will do anything to get a kick.

Mr. Justice Stanbery:

Where were the police at this time?

Mr. Smith:

I don't know, Your Honor. Perhaps they were out giving parking tickets. There is no doubt that the drug laws are unevenly enforced. A youngster usually gets caught by accident. This is another reason why the laws against marijuana are unworkable and should be struck down. They provide the police with the perfect tool to harass people whom they consider to be undesirables.

Marijuana, as it is commonly smoked in this country, is just not harmful and there is no reason to ban it. As I've already stated, the government could, of course, regulate cannabis use, and government regulation should be combined with education. If the recent experience with LSD proves anything, most people don't want to harm themselves. People use marijuana because they know that it does not adversely affect their mental processes and that it does not harm them physically. All marijuana does is make a person high for a few hours during which his senses are heightened and his inner vision seems to be expanded. People who prefer to achieve relaxation and enjoyment in this manner should be free to do so. They have a constitutional right to be let alone.

As has been said by this Court, in another context, the Constitution was designed to take the government off the backs of the people. We submit that an individual's private pursuit of pleasure is beyond the pale of governmental prohibition. The decision in the *Stanley* case, where the Court held that the people who get kicks from dirty movies should be free to do so in the privacy of their homes, supports that proposition. Similarly here, people who get their kicks from marijuana should be free to do so in the privacy of their own homes as long as they don't harm themselves or anyone else.

THE CHIEF JUSTICE:

As long as you are on that subject, how do you respond to the contention that the use of marijuana leads to criminal activity or sexual aberrations?

MR. SMITH:

While some persons who use marijuana may commit crimes, people who drink water also commit crimes.

MR. JUSTICE STANBERY:

That begs the question.

MR. SMITH:

No, if the Court please. There is no evidence that the use of marijuana causes criminality. This has been borne out by everybody who has studied the situation. For example, the LaGuardia committee found that there was no proof that marijuana use was connected with the commission of crime or that it led to increased sexuality. This has been consistently recognized. The New York County Medical Society and the President's Commission on Law Enforcement and the Administration of Justice have both found absolutely no evidence to indicate that marijuana causes criminal behavior. First of all, as I noted earlier, marijuana is not physically addictive, so the user has no habit to support. Thus, the prime reason for criminal activity among narcotic addicts is missing with marijuana. Second, unlike alcohol, which releases aggression and quite frequently induces antisocial behavior and has been indicated as a major factor in the commission of serious crimes of violence, marijuana quiets the user and makes him more introspective. Thus, as the undercover investigators for the LaGuardia committee discovered when they visited the tea pads, marijuana users are a very quiet lot.

Another relevant example is the experience at the folk-rock festivals. At the Woodstock Festival in 1969, for instance, it was estimated that over 90 percent of the audience openly smoked marijuana, but there were no antisocial incidents to speak of. The police chief of Beverly Hills, who went to Woodstock to observe, noted that he had never seen so many people in such a small area act so peacefully. One could easily imagine what would have happened if they had been drinking liquor.

Even H. J. Anslinger, former head of the Bureau of Narcotics, who was one of the prime movers to get marijuana banned, noted before a congressional subcommittee in the 1950s that marijuana was not a "controlling factor in the commission of crimes." As summed up by Dr. Stanley F. Yolles in his testimony before a congressional subcommittee in February of 1970, "Persons under the influence of marijuana tend to be passive. It is true that sometimes a crime may be committed by a person while under the influence of marijuana. However, any drug which loosens one's self-control is likely to do the same and relates primarily to the personality of the user."

MR. JUSTICE WOODWARD:

But he just said that crimes may be committed by persons under the influence of marijuana.

MR. SMITH:

Yes, but that wouldn't be the normal person.

MR. JUSTICE WOODWARD:

It matters very little to the person who is hit over the head that his assailant was abnormal and that the violent outburst was merely triggered—and not caused—by marijuana. While reading the briefs that were filed, I noted that your adversary cited a report by Dr. Walter Bromberg, who was senior psychiatrist at Bellevue Hospital for many years, in which he asserted that marijuana can "breed" crime in the sense that if it is used by psychopathic types, it allows the emergence of their latent aggressive or antisocial tendencies. Perhaps it was that one marijuana cigarette which triggered the Licata boy's homicidal mania.

MR. SMITH:

That was all some forty years ago and, when marijuana was involved, everyone assumed that it was the trigger; inquiry then ceased. The fact of the matter is, however, that causation has not been proved, and that the Constitution does not permit governmental interference with people's private pursuit of pleasure on the basis of mere speculation. Indeed, both the President's Commission on Law Enforcement and the Administration of Justice and the British Advisory Committee on Drug Dependence note that the circumstantial evidence link between marijuana and crime is much weaker than the known link between alcohol and crime. Similarly, studies in Brazil and Nigeria have failed to find a causal relationship between cannabis and criminal activities.

MR. JUSTICE PECKHAM:

Assuming for the moment that you are correct and that marijuana is not harmful in and of itself, isn't there an indication that marijuana users do graduate to the dangerous hard drugs?

MR. SMITH:

I think that the statistics are extremely misleading. While it is true that studies do show that a majority of heroin addicts have previously used marijuana, they also show that very few marijuana users go on to heroin. The LaGuardia committee specifically found that marijuana, which is not addictive and is not dangerous, does *not* lead to the use of dangerous or addictive drugs. There is nothing in the scientific properties of marijuana that would cause a marijuana smoker to use any of the hard drugs. What has happened, however, is that the stiff criminal penalties for possession and use of marijuana have forced people who otherwise would be free to purchase their marijuana openly to resort to a criminal supply. This exposes them to heroin and the other dangerous drugs. Pushers would like nothing better than to get a kid hooked on heroin. Heroin habits are very expensive to maintain, and the addict gives the pusher a good steady source of income. Marijuana, on the other hand, is non-addictive and is much cheaper than heroin. If marijuana is legalized, people will not be forced to resort to an underground supply and will have less exposure to the hard narcotics.

Another reason some marijuana users experiment with other drugs is that they don't believe the Establishment when it tells them that they are dangerous. They hear all the time how harmful marijuana is, but they know, from their own experience, that it simply isn't so. If the government would only admit that marijuana is not harmful—something that the marijuana user already knows—then people will believe the government when it says that heroin or LSD is dangerous.

In any event, as I said before, scientific studies have shown that there is nothing inherent in the physical properties of marijuana that would lead users to the hard narcotics. The basic textbook on pharmacology, Goodman and Gilman's *The Pharmacological Basis of Therapeutics,* states quite explicitly that marijuana use does not lead to the use of heroin. Now, of course, there may be some people who are predisposed to use heroin just as they were predisposed to use marijuana, but these people would use heroin even if marijuana were nonexistent. In fact, evidence has shown that marijuana users on the college campuses and others who are not in heroin-risk environments do not become heroin addicts. The real question to ask is not how many people who use heroin have also used marijuana, but how many people who use marijuana go on to use heroin. Dr. Yolles estimates that less than 5 percent of the chronic marijuana users go on to use heroin. This is a very small figure indeed.

Not only is it clear that marijuana use does not lead to the use of heroin, but there is even some evidence that marijuana use may be a substitute for heroin addiction. One type of person who craves a mind-altering drug will use anything that is available, whether it is marijuana, heroin, or LSD. For example, during the short-lived effectiveness of Operation Intercept in 1969, which closed the Mexican border to marijuana so that it became very scarce, New York City authorities reported that heroin sales increased. Marijuana serves as a harmless outlet for those who seem to need some form of mind-altering substance.

THE CHIEF JUSTICE:

Are you saying that we should legalize marijuana because it is, in effect, the lesser of two evils?

MR. SMITH:

Not at all, Mr. Chief Justice. I am only saying that marijuana use does not lead to the use of heroin. Furthermore, as I have already pointed out, marijuana use does not harm the individual nor does it make him dangerous to society. I would not ask that it be legalized because it is the lesser of two evils. I am asking that it be legalized because it is not an evil.

MR. JUSTICE BRADFORD:

Mr. Smith, you have been telling us that marijuana doesn't adversely affect either the mental or the physical health of the user. It is true, however, is it not, that marijuana is used by many people to withdraw from the realities of life—to escape its hardships and disappointments? Isn't this harmful to society as a whole, if not to the individual?

MR. SMITH:

It is used by some as a vehicle for escape, just as some use alcohol for that purpose. Others use marijuana to relax and as a social amenity, in the same way the cocktail is used. Still others use it because it increases their sensory awareness and gives them greater insight into themselves and the world in which they live.

MR. JUSTICE BRADFORD:

Whether you call it relaxation or not, this state induced by marijuana still tends to remove people from the mainstream of thought and activity, and people who cannot cope with problems of everyday life will use marijuana as a crutch. Is that not correct?

MR. SMITH:

There are people, of course, who would use any

57

mind-altering drug to escape the problems of the real world.

MR. JUSTICE SPENCER:

Then marijuana is a mind-altering drug?

MR. SMITH:

Of course it is. I've never denied that. People have been using mind-altering drugs since time immemorial. Our own society is full of mind-altering drugs and not only condones their use, but encourages it. Ten minutes can't go by without the television viewer's being subjected to advertisements that seek to sell him products that will relax him, pep him up, put him to sleep, or keep him awake. We drink liquor, smoke tobacco, and take pills all in an attempt either to escape from the rigors of life or to find something that will assist us in meeting them. It is estimated that there are some five million people who use amphetamines and barbiturates and that the sedative and tranquilizing drugs comprise some 17 to 20 percent of all medical prescriptions. Furthermore, even the supposedly innocuous cola drinks contain a substance called theobromine, which is a mild stimulant from cacao beans and kola nuts, and which, together with the caffeine these drinks contain, is perhaps why people get a lift when they drink them.

There is no doubt that marijuana can be and is being used not only as a means of achieving a heightened sensory awareness but also as a pleasant way of temporarily forgetting about the cares of the world. But there is one difference between marijuana and some of the other "crutches" used in our society. Tobacco cigarettes cause lung cancer and heart disease; alcohol incapacitates millions—there are some five million alcoholics in this country and, as I have noted earlier, 20 percent of the patients admitted to state mental hospitals were admitted because of alcoholic problems; marijuana, on the other hand, is harmless. Certainly, it distorts time perception somewhat and may interfere with coherent thinking while the person is under its influence, as does alcohol. But marijuana does not have all the side effects of alcohol—it does not leave a hangover, it does not kill.

MR. JUSTICE BRADFORD:

Wouldn't it be dangerous to permit adolescents to use marijuana? Might not it keep them from mentally maturing, from being able to cope properly with the real world? If young people can use marijuana to find an easy way out of their troubles, they will never be able to face the very real problems of growing up. Just as the butterfly has to struggle to get out of the cocoon or else it will be too weak to survive, so it is with young people. If marijuana makes life appear to be easy or if it provides too easy a way out, youngsters will never be able to survive. Marijuana may well produce generations of lost souls.

MR. SMITH:

We do not condone the use of marijuana by minors. Minors are not allowed to buy alcohol; the government can provide that they should not be allowed to buy marijuana.

MR. JUSTICE BRADFORD:

In practical terms though, how can this be enforced? Teen-agers have no trouble getting liquor today if they really want it.

MR. SMITH:

If the Court please, they have even less trouble getting marijuana. Marijuana can be obtained only through illegal channels, and it matters little to the seller whether he sells to a minor or to an adult.

MR. JUSTICE WOODWARD:

Aren't the penalties much greater for the sale of marijuana to minors than to adults?

MR. SMITH:

Yes, Your Honor, but the penalties on sales of marijuana to adults are also harsh. The seller just doesn't expect to get caught. It's that same psychology which prompts us all to speed on the highway—we don't think it will happen to us. My point is, however, that it is presently easier for an adolescent to purchase marijuana than it is for him to purchase alcohol. If marijuana were legalized, people could purchase their marijuana openly from established or even licensed sellers, and the illicit traffic would fade away. Under such conditions, it would be much more difficult for the minor to obtain marijuana. He would still be able to get it, but it would be more difficult. But you see, he is getting it now, even though it is illegal, and at the same time he is being exposed to a criminal element.

MR. JUSTICE SPENCER:

Shouldn't these arguments be made to Congress

and to the various state legislatures rather than
to us?

MR. SMITH:

There is so much misinformation concerning marijuana that it would be impossible to get Congress
or the state legislatures to legalize marijuana.

MR. JUSTICE SPENCER:

Nothing is impossible. Morris Sheppard, who was
a United States senator from Texas and the author
of the Eighteenth Amendment, once commented
that there was as much chance of repealing prohibition as there was for a hummingbird to fly to
the planet Mars with the Washington Monument
tied to its tail. And yet, less than fifteen years after
it was ratified, the Eighteenth Amendment was
repealed. If marijuana is being used by as many
people as you say, and the children of our public
officials, including the children of a couple of our
senators, are being arrested for the possession of
marijuana, perhaps political pressure will force legalization. I've noticed that there are efforts under
way to reduce the penalties for mere possession.
Why isn't that the proper solution?

MR. SMITH:

It is one solution, Your Honor. But, citizens should
not have to wait for the legislatures to restore their
constitutional rights. This Court has never hesi-
tated to strike down legislation that deprives people
of their fundamental liberties. The laws prohibiting the private possession and use of marijuana are
unwarranted intrusions into people's private affairs.
This Court should not wait for legislative action

here, just as it did not wait for those states that had segregated schools to desegregate them.

THE CHIEF JUSTICE:

You admitted a while ago that marijuana causes sensory distortion and can impair the judgment, if only temporarily, of the user. Why doesn't this make it dangerous for the marijuana user to drive an automobile or operate machinery, and why isn't this a sufficient reason for upholding the constitutionality of its prohibition?

MR. SMITH:

First, as I've already indicated, Drs. Zinberg and Weil, who conducted those experiments at Boston University, report that marijuana has little influence on the centers that control the mechanical aspects of speech or muscular coordination.

THE CHIEF JUSTICE:

Yes, but marijuana does adversely affect that portion of the brain which controls thought and perception.

MR. SMITH:

That's true, Mr. Chief Justice. Marijuana can influence the thought processes, allowing people to become more introspective. It gives them a greater feeling of awareness. It also modifies perception.

THE CHIEF JUSTICE:

Doesn't this make it difficult and exceedingly dangerous for the person under the influence of marijuana to drive?

MR. SMITH:

It probably would. But it is similarly dangerous to drive under the influence of many substances that are freely available today. Many cold remedies available with or without a prescription contain warnings on their labels that the person who takes the medicine should not drive. Alcohol, which is freely available, is a leading, if not *the* leading, factor in automobile accidents, and yet this is not deemed to be sufficient reason for prohibiting its possession.

MR. JUSTICE SPENCER:

Well, surely the legislature doesn't have to prohibit all dangerous substances if it decides to prohibit one, does it?

MR. SMITH:

No, Mr. Justice Spencer, but we submit that if there are two substances used for the same purpose and one is no more harmful, and in fact may be less harmful, than the other, the legislature cannot ban one without banning the other. To do so would be to discriminate against those who seek to use the prohibited substance and would deny them equal protection of the laws. With the Court's permission, I will explore this aspect of our argument later.

We submit, however, that marijuana does not impair driving skills as much as alcohol, and while I would not like to be driven around by one under the influence of marijuana, I would prefer that to being driven around by someone who was drunk. In the late 1960s an interesting experiment was conducted by the director of research of the Department of Motor Vehicles in Olympia, Washington. He compared the driving skills of people who were under the influence of marijuana (who had smoked enough to achieve a normal social high) with those of people who had a .10 percent alcohol concentration in their blood—which was the legally-defined level of intoxication. The test was a controlled laboratory experiment.

MR. JUSTICE WOODWARD:
You mean it was not conducted under actual driving conditions?

MR. SMITH:
That's correct, Your Honor. The volunteers were carefully screened, and those who were finally selected were separated into three groups. The first group smoked marijuana until they reached an acceptable social high.

MR. JUSTICE WOODWARD:
How was this determined?

MR. SMITH:
The subjects were experienced marijuana users. As I have noted earlier, marijuana smokers who have had some experience with the substance know how much to take in order to reach their desired state of high. Also, unlike the case of one who is intoxicated with alcohol, it is almost impossible to tell if a person is under the influence of marijuana just by looking at him. Therefore, the researchers also measured the subjects' pulse rate in order to confirm that they were indeed under the influence of marijuana. The second group of subjects was given drinks that were 95 percent alcohol—190 proof—until its members' blood showed an alcohol concentration of .10 percent. The third group was the

control, and its members were given neither marijuana nor alcohol. All these groups drove a simulator that was connected to a screen upon which was projected a twenty-three-minute film of actual traffic situations. They had to steer, brake, and accelerate as they would if they were actually driving.

The experimenters found that those subjects who were under the influence of marijuana showed less impairment in their skills than did those who were at the legal level of intoxication. They further found that increasing the dose of marijuana did not have any significant effect. Now, while this test was not conducted under actual driving conditions, so that the actual stress felt when driving a real automobile was not present, it did show that, at least in the neutral setting of the laboratory, marijuana had less of an adverse effect upon basic driving skills than did alcohol. Of course, the third group, which was not under the influence of either marijuana or alcohol, did best of all on the driving simulator.

I will concede that people who are under the influence of marijuana are not as good drivers as those who are not—but that is no reason to prohibit its possession and use. At most, this is a collateral problem to the marijuana issue, just as it is a collateral problem to the alcohol issue. As the late Mr. Justice Brandeis said, "Among free men, the deterrents ordinarily to be applied to prevent crime are education and punishment for violations of the law." Driving while under the influence of marijuana can be discouraged by education and

Ralph Adam Fine

can be deterred by making it a crime. But the private possession and use of marijuana cannot be prevented merely because some might misuse it.

It is an axiom of the law that prohibitions upon the freedom of individuals must be no broader than that which is absolutely necessary to accomplish some valid legislative purpose. Thus, for example, in the Connecticut contraceptive case, Connecticut's stated purpose of discouraging premarital and extramarital promiscuous conduct could not provide constitutional support for a statute that prohibited married couples from using contraceptives, because the statute intruded upon the privacy of marriage. Similarly, in the pornographic film case, this Court held that Georgia's stated purpose in preventing sex crimes could not provide constitutional support for a statute that also intruded upon the privacy of the individual in his own home. Thus, if a state passed a law prohibiting the possession of automobiles because unlicensed people may drive them, or if some states passed laws prohibiting the possession of sugar or soft drinks because overuse causes cavities and sugar adversely affects diabetics, I am sure that this Court would strike such legislation down.

MR. JUSTICE WOODWARD:
Didn't we say in *Stanley* v. *Georgia* that the decision should not be interpreted to infringe upon the power of the government to make possession of other items, such as narcotics, firearms, or stolen goods, a crime?

MR. SMITH:
Yes, Your Honor.

66

MR. JUSTICE WOODWARD:

Why wouldn't marijuana come within that proviso or its rationale?

MR. SMITH:

There is no constitutional objection, as I see the law, to a state's making criminal the possession of items that can be used only to harm others or the user. Thus, the possession of machine guns may properly be prohibited, as may the possession of heroin. There is no legitimate use for the machine gun, and the use of heroin is harmful. But, the use of marijuana is not, and people should be allowed to use it.

MR. JUSTICE KING:

I have noticed in your recitation of the various experiments that you emphasized that the researchers always screened out as possible subjects those people who had prior histories of psychological troubles or whose response to psychological questionnaires indicated they might be prone to psychotic reactions. Are the experiments really valid then? You are asking to have marijuana legalized. Legalization will make marijuana available to everyone, not just to those who have passed a battery of psychological tests. Isn't this sufficient justification for the legislative prohibition?

MR. SMITH:

I don't think so, Your Honor. This Court has made it clear many times that the extrasensitivity of some members of society to something is insufficient reason to forbid its use by everyone. Obscenity is a good example. It is clear that the sale or public display of obscene material is not protected by the

First Amendment and thus can be prohibited, as opposed to the private possession and viewing of obscenity, which cannot be prohibited, as this Court has held in the *Stanley* case. But, in deciding what is and what is not obscene, this Court has said that the material must be measured against current community standards. Thus, while some persons might conceivably be erotically aroused by advertisements for women's apparel or, for that matter, by sexually explicit movies and books—even to the extent that they might commit antisocial acts as a result of the exposure to such materials—this Court has decided that their individual quirks, if you will, cannot be the bases for prohibition. Additionally, as I have already noted, diabetics can't tolerate too much sugar and salt is bad for people with heart conditions, but their sensibilities cannot be used as a basis for depriving others of these substances.

THE CHIEF JUSTICE:

But salt and sugar are necessities, and people who have to restrict their intake of these items know so and can voluntarily protect themselves. Marijuana is not a necessity and it can harm precisely those people who are powerless to protect themselves—people who are already psychologically disturbed.

MR. SMITH:

Sexually arousing books and movies are not necessities either, and the person who is predisposed to commit sexually-oriented crimes because of his exposure to such material will not be able to walk by the bookstore or movie theater either. This is the risk that a free society must take, however, in ensuring freedom for all. Let me reemphasize, though, that one of the preeminent researchers in this field, Dr. Zinberg, has stated that true acute psychotic reactions in marijuana users are rare, and he has labeled them "psychiatric curiosities."

MR. JUSTICE SPENCER:

Your analogy to so-called obscenity disturbs me. Reading matter or films are specifically protected by the First Amendment, which prohibits Congress and the states from making any law abridging the freedom of speech or of the press. There is no constitutional right to smoke marijuana. It simply doesn't exist.

MR. JUSTICE BADGER:

Mr. Smith, doesn't the Ninth Amendment recognize guarantees to personal liberty despite the lack of any specific provision when it declares that the "enumeration in the Constitution, of certain rights, shall not be construed to deny or disparage others retained by the people"?

MR. SMITH:

Yes, Your Honor, and we submit that this includes the right to be alone, the right to be free from unwarranted governmental interference. And if the government cannot demonstrate that some legitimate and compelling social purpose is served by an intrusion into the private affairs of its citizens, then that intrusion is unwarranted and unconstitutional.

We also submit that the laws that prohibit the private possession and the personal use of marijuana unconstitutionally discriminate against a very large class of people. I agree that marijuana is a mind-altering substance. Depending upon the personality of the user, marijuana may, as the President's Commission on Law Enforcement and the Administration of Justice noted, induce exaltation, joyousness, and hilarity or it may induce quietude and reveries. It may also produce sharp color hallucinations, and the user may be disoriented as to time and space. Millions of Americans smoke marijuana because they find these sensations enjoyable.

Alcohol is also a mind-altering substance and similarly may induce exaltation, joyousness, and hilarity. People who become intoxicated from liquor may see hallucinations and are frequently disoriented as to time and space. Millions of Americans who drink liquor do so because they also find these sensations to be enjoyable. Alcohol, however, has other, more harmful, effects upon the human body. The person who drinks alcohol will have impaired physical coordination that becomes greater as the alcoholic concentration in his blood increases, until finally he dies. Furthermore, heavy long-term drinking causes a variety of serious physical and mental ailments and can also lead to death. As I have pointed out, all this is simply not true with marijuana. Scientific studies have consistently indicated that marijuana does not seriously adversely affect the user, either in the short term or in the long term.

MR. JUSTICE BRADFORD:
Getting back to what you said about impaired physical coordination, I thought it was agreed that, by distorting the senses, marijuana can have the same

adverse effect on the performance of various tasks, for example driving, as does alcohol.

MR. SMITH:

Not exactly, Mr. Justice Bradford. As I've indicated, marijuana does not impair mechanical skills, such as are required for driving, to the same degree as alcohol. Although it does affect the judgment of the driver—as does alcohol—it leaves coordination and the reflexes comparatively intact. Thus, a driver under the influence of alcohol not only may not want to drive safely, he cannot. A person under the influence of marijuana, however, may not want to drive safely, if that's his mood at the moment, but he is nonetheless physically able to do so if he wishes.

Now, not only can alcohol adversely affect the individual drinker, but it also incapacitates millions and, because it tends to release formerly inhibited aggressions, alcohol also adversely affects society. The British Council on Alcoholism estimates, for example, that some 250,000 British workers stay home from work on Mondays to recover from their weekends of indulgence. In this country, alcohol-associated absenteeism costs industry over two billion dollars a year.

Alcohol is also an important factor in the commission of serious crimes. It has been estimated that in over half of all the crimes of violence, the perpetrators had been drinking. As I explained earlier, this is not the case with marijuana.

MR. JUSTICE STANBERY:

Why does it necessarily follow that alcohol has caused the criminal behavior? If I remember correctly, you argued very strenuously before that similar statistics with respect to marijuana and crime did not prove anything because there was no casual relationship. What makes you so sure that there is a causal relationship between alcohol and crime?

MR. SMITH:

The nature of the beast, Your Honor. As the LaGuardia committee researchers found, marijuana quiets people and makes them more reflective. On the other hand, while alcohol may also quiet some people, it generally serves to weaken their inhibitions and may make them violent and unruly. This difference in reactions produced by marijuana and alcohol is illustrated by this old tale:

One night, three men arrived at the closed gates of a Persian city. One was intoxicated by alcohol, another was under the spell of opium, and the third was steeped in marijuana. The first blustered, "Let's break the gates down." "Nay," yawned the opium eater, "let us rest until morning when we may enter through the wide-flung portals." "Do as you like," announced the marijuana user, "but I shall stroll in through the keyhole."

Alcohol also causes the dissolution of many marriages, with the attendant evils not only to the individuals concerned but to society as well. It is estimated that alcohol is the main factor in 75 percent of the domestic-relations actions brought into court. Many other unfortunate couples endure their liquor-induced marital difficulties without seeking judicial relief.

In sum, it is clear that alcohol is more harmful to both society and the individual than is marijuana. And yet, while alcohol is a legal means for people to seek relaxation and enjoyment and even to escape from the troubles of the world, marijuana is not. This arbitrary classification is without rational basis and unfairly discriminates against marijuana devotees. They have been denied the equal protection of the laws guaranteed by the Fourteenth Amendment to the Constitution.

The leading authority for the proposition that states cannot give disparate treatment to people whose circumstances do not intrinsically differ is the 1942 decision of *Skinner* v. *Oklahoma*. That case concerned an Oklahoma statute which provided for the sterilization of "habitual criminals." Habitual criminals were defined by the statute as being persons who, having twice been convicted of felonies involving moral turpitude, were convicted a third time and imprisoned. Excluded from felonies deemed to involve moral turpitude were various white-collar crimes such as embezzlement. Skinner had been convicted three times for committing felonies involving moral turpitude, one of these convictions being for the crime of stealing chickens, and he was to be sterilized pursuant to court order. He appealed to this Court, which held that the Oklahoma sterilization law violated the Fourteenth Amendment's guarantee of equal protection of the laws because the seemingly artificial classifications exempted some felons from the operation of the statute while consigning others to the surgeon's knife. Unable to find a distinction between chicken stealing and embezzlement that would warrant sterilizing those who committed the first type of crime but not the latter, the Court noted that Oklahoma had laid "an unequal hand on those who had committed intrinsically the same quality of offense," and the Court pointed out that this was prohibited by the Constitution. Similarly here, the marijuana laws lay an unequal hand on those who seek pleasure and relaxation. The marijuana user is imprisoned; the liquor drinker is not.

MR. JUSTICE BADGER:

If I remember correctly, didn't we base the decision on the ground that sterilization destroys a fundamental civil right of man—the right to procreate?

MR. SMITH:

You did, Your Honor. But I submit that the right to be free is also one of the fundamental rights of man, and that right cannot be taken away by the imposition of uneven-handed laws. When the person who derives his pleasure from marijuana is locked up for five, ten, or twenty years, or even a day, while those who get their kicks from alcohol are not, then, I submit, the marijuana smoker is being denied the equal protection of the laws.

THE CHIEF JUSTICE:

Is there any constitutional necessity for the legislature to punish all evils or none at all? For example, if the legislature did not prohibit or punish the sale of adulterated bread, couldn't it still prohibit and punish the sale of adulterated milk without the consequence of one who was violating the latter prohibition claiming immunity from prosecution because the other purveyors of poisoned food products were not punished?

MR. SMITH:

I think that might be a very close question, Mr. Chief Justice. The fact that the legislature seemed to be preferring one class of wrongdoer over another might very well invalidate the statute. For example, in *McLaughlin* v. *Florida,* this Court held that a Florida statute which made it a crime for an unmarried interracial couple, but not an unmarried couple of the same race, to share the same bedroom at night denied the persons who were convicted under that statute equal protection of the laws precisely because the legislature took one activity that it believed to be wrong and against the public interest—that is, unmarried people sharing the same bedroom at night—and did not prohibit everyone from doing it.

In Your Honor's example, it could be argued that when the legislature acted against an activity that it believed to be wrong—that is, the selling of adulterated food—it should have prohibited that activity entirely, and without distinguishing between items. But this Court need not deal with that question here, for the laws against the use and possession of narcotics and marijuana are founded upon the proposition that the prohibited substances are harmful to the user and dangerous to society. There can be no doubt that heroin and the other narcotics are much more dangerous to society than alcohol. There is no uneven application of the unequal laws there. But, when a state includes marijuana in the list of prohibited substances because of a mistaken belief that it harms the user, causes him to commit crimes, and the like, and these reasons are not supported by substantial scientific evidence, that prohibition must fall. Where in fact marijuana is less dangerous than alcohol, the government cannot allow people to use alcohol yet bar the marijuana route to pleasure. Just as in the appropriately named case of *Loving* v. *Virginia,* where this Court struck down a law prohibiting interracial marriage because it violated the constitutional command that people be treated equally, so here too, I submit, people should be free to seek pleasure without having their pursuit blocked by invalid and unreasonable distinctions.

MR. JUSTICE SPENCER:

Isn't that argument better made to the legislatures of the respective states? The *Loving* and *McLaughlin* cases held that distinctions based on race were invidious and could not be squared with the Fourteenth Amendment's mandate of equal protection, but I don't see how you can classify the distinctions between marijuana and alcohol as invidious. It is a judgment made by the legislature.

MR. SMITH:

As I noted earlier, the legislatures of many states similarly made judgments that Negroes were inferior to whites and decreed that they should go to separate schools, but this Court, in *Brown* v. *Board of Education,* looked at the evidence and said:

Nonsense—and forbade the states from imposing segregation.

MR. JUSTICE SPENCER:

But in the *Loving* and *McLaughlin* and *Brown* cases, the classifications were invidious because they were based on race. There is no such invidious race-based classification here.

MR. SMITH:

That's correct, Your Honor. But I think that the teachings of those cases have broader application. The 1968 case of *Levy* v. *Louisiana* is also significant. There, Louisiana denied illegitimate children the right to recover damages for the wrongful death of their mother on the ground that such a rule discouraged bringing children into the world out of wedlock. While agreeing that this was a socially desirable aim, this Court decided that Louisiana could not provide to legitimate children a remedy for the wrongful death of their parents yet deny that remedy to illegitimate children.

Here, the government has determined to allow the use of certain substances that are employed solely as pleasure-inducing agents. It cannot pick and choose, permitting some but not others, without any rational reason. The scientific evidence clearly demonstrates that marijuana is less dangerous than alcohol, and therefore there is no rational reason to ban marijuana alone. It should not be prohibited.

So far this morning I have tried to demonstrate that in normal usage marijuana is not harmful to the user and is not dangerous to society. Thus, there is no compelling reason for the government to outlaw marijuana, thereby infringing upon the privacy of the people in their personal pursuit of pleasure. By the same token, because marijuana is not harmful and is in fact less dangerous than alcohol, the government cannot show any reasonable basis for prohibiting the one and not the other. By outlawing marijuana and imposing penalties for its possession, it thus unconstitutionally discriminates against those who seek pleasure through the use of marijuana.

There is, however, another reason why Rodriguez' conviction must be reversed. He has been sentenced to imprisonment for the mere possession of marijuana. He did not smoke it, he did not sell it, he merely possessed it. We respectfully submit that to impose this penalty for mere possession, and nothing more, is to impose cruel and unusual punishment in violation of the Eighth Amendment to the Constitution. This proposition is directly supported by *Robinson* v. *California,* decided by this Court in 1962.

California law made it a crime to be addicted to the use of narcotics. The state merely had to show that a person was an addict when he was found within its borders. It did not have to show actual use of narcotics inside the state, just mere addiction. Robinson was spotted on the street by some Los Angeles police officers who noticed the telltale needle marks and scars on his left arm. He was arrested, tried, and convicted for being an addict within the state of California and was sentenced to ninety days' imprisonment. He was convicted merely for being an addict, and not for having used narcotics. This Court held that imposing criminal punishment for mere status, without a showing of use, disorderly conduct, or other antisocial behavior, was an imposition of a cruel and unusual punishment, in violation of the Eighth Amendment to the Constitution. The Court noted that Robinson's sentence of ninety days was not, in the abstract, cruel and unusual but held that to deprive someone of his liberty for even one day as a punishment for status would be within the constitutional prohibition.

Similarly here, Rodriguez has been punished by imprisonment merely because he had the status at the time of his arrest of a "possessor" of marijuana. There was absolutely no proof whatever that he intended to use it or sell it. In fact, he testified that he had never in his life smoked marijuana.

MR. JUSTICE WOODWARD:
Why did he keep the marijuana when it was given to him, if he didn't intend to at least try it? He could have thrown the cigarettes away.

MR. SMITH:
The gas station was very busy and I guess he didn't have time. Also, he testified that he was somewhat curious to see what marijuana looked like.

MR. JUSTICE WOODWARD:
Do you think that this curiosity would have led him to try it?

MR. SMITH:
He testified that he had never smoked marijuana

in his life because he thought it was harmful, and for that reason I don't think he would have tried it. But, of course, this is not my judgment to make— nor can the Court make this judgment now. The state introduced no evidence at all that Rodriguez intended to use the marijuana. They have the burden of proof in criminal trials, but they introduced no evidence at all. They chose simply to prove possession.

But I think that *Robinson* stands for the proposition that mere possession is not enough—there must be some link with, or a threat of, actual anti-social activity. As Mr. Justice Marshall said in *Powell* v. *Texas,* where the Court upheld Powell's conviction for public drunkenness despite his claim that under the doctrine of *Robinson* v. *California* he was being impermissibly punished for a crime of status: "The State of Texas has not sought to punish a mere status, as California did in *Robinson;* nor has it attempted to regulate appellant's behavior in the privacy of his own home. Rather, it has imposed upon appellant a criminal sanction for public behavior which may create substantial health and safety hazards, both for appellant and members of the general public, and which offends the moral and aesthetic sensibility of a large segment of the community." Here, Rodriguez is not being punished for public behavior which may create a substantial health and safety hazard. He is being punished merely for possessing two marijuana cigarettes. I respectfully submit that this case is controlled by the *Robinson* decision and that any punishment of Rodriguez for mere possession violates the Eighth Amendment's prohibition against the imposition of cruel and unusual punishment.

In sum, it is our position that the laws which ban the personal possession or use of marijuana are unconstitutional, and I respectfully submit that the judgment of the Supreme Court of Pennsylvania should be reversed.

I would like to reserve the remainder of my time for rebuttal.

PART THREE

Argument on Behalf of the
Commonwealth of
Pennsylvania

THE CHIEF JUSTICE:

Mr. Peters.

MR. PETERS:

Mr. Chief Justice and may it please the Court. I agree with Mr. Justice Badger that this case is a pretty big nutshell. It is a nutshell, if I may carry the analogy one step further, whose meat contains the poison of misdirected liberality. Rodriguez is asking this Court—in the name of liberty—to legalize a drug—a mind-altering drug and a hallucinogenic drug—about which we know very little and which may be very dangerous indeed.

Now, Rodriguez has based most of his argument on the notion that somehow there is a constitutional right to smoke marijuana and that laws which prohibit the possession of marijuana violate his right to privacy. I respectfully submit that there is no constitutional right of privacy broad enough to cover the possession and use of marijuana. There can be no doubt that a state may prohibit the manufacture or sale of harmful products. By the same token, it may prohibit people from possessing these harmful products. This Court has continuously upheld the power of the government to prohibit the possession of noxious materials as a necessary adjunct to the banning of their manufacture or sale. For example, in *Crane* v. *Campbell,* this Court rejected contentions that Idaho's law banning the possession of liquor in that state's so-called dry districts violated the Constitution. The Court noted that inasmuch as alcohol was a potentially harmful substance, Idaho had the constitutional power to prohibit its manufacture or sale within its borders. The ban on personal possession was upheld because it was part and parcel of the suppression of illegal traffic in alcohol.

Furthermore, it does not matter that certain individuals may not be adversely affected by a substance deemed to be harmful to the public at large. In *Samuels* v. *McCurdy,* this Court held that the law prohibiting the personal possession of alcohol was constitutional even though the alcohol was for private consumption only. The Court noted that since the laws that prohibited the manufacture, sale, or possession of liquor were reasonably designed to protect people and society from its adverse effects, a state could, consistent with the Constitution, forbid possession by everyone, including those who might not be susceptible to harm.

In both cases, the Court recognized that the personal possession of alcohol for private use was "not one of those fundamental privileges" protected by the Constitution. Similarly, we submit that the personal possession of marijuana is not one of those fundamental privileges protected by the Constitution and that it may be prohibited entirely. Additionally, we submit that the ban on the personal possession of marijuana, even if that marijuana is to be used for private consumption only, is necessary to maintain effective controls on this potentially harmful drug.

MR. JUSTICE BADGER:

When were *Crane* and *Samuels* decided?

MR. PETERS:

Crane was decided in 1917 and *Samuels* in 1925.

MR. JUSTICE BADGER:

Don't you think that we have progressed somewhat since then in our views of the scope of the Constitution's protection of liberty?

MR. PETERS:

We have, Your Honor.

MR. JUSTICE BRADFORD:

Counselor, aren't you really saying that the Constitution prohibits only specific intrusions upon liberties such as unreasonable searches and seizures, limitations on the freedom of speech, and the like?

MR. PETERS:

Yes, Mr. Justice Bradford.

MR. JUSTICE BRADFORD:

And that the so-called right of privacy encompasses only those areas that are already protected by some fundamental guarantee found in the Constitution?

MR. PETERS:

Precisely, Your Honor.

MR. JUSTICE WOODWARD:

How do you distinguish *Griswold* v. *Connecticut* and *Stanley* v. *Georgia?*

MR. PETERS:

The Georgia obscenity case merely held that the government has no right to control the thoughts of its citizens, freedom of thought being a right that stems from the First Amendment's protection of freedom of speech. The Court specifically noted, however, that the decision did not infringe upon the power of the states to make illegal the possession of other items not within the ambit of the First Amendment's protection.

The Connecticut contraceptive case merely reaffirmed people's right to a certain degree of familial or marital privacy. This right, although admittedly not stemming from any specific constitutional guarantee, was thought to evolve naturally from the Bill of Rights taken as a whole. It was an extension of earlier decisions of this Court upholding the right of parents to control, to a certain extent at least, the upbringing of their children. Parents have the right to send their children to private schools if they wish and have the right to have them learn foreign languages if they wish. *Griswold* merely upheld the right of married people to procreate or not to procreate, as they wish, and as the Court pointed out in the *Skinner* case, relied on by my adversary, the right to bear children is a fundamental human right. But I don't think that, by any stretch of the imagination, the right to smoke pot can be classified among the fundamental rights of mankind.

MR. JUSTICE CUSHING:

Wouldn't you say that whether a right is classified as "fundamental" or not—and here we are really just using words—a state cannot arbitrarily run people's lives? For example, there is no right as such to drink cherry soda rather than ginger ale, but I don't think that a state could forbid people from imbibing cherry soda if they wished to.

MR. PETERS:

Unless, of course, the state had reason to believe that cherry soda was harmful—then I don't think there is any doubt that the state could ban it.

MR. JUSTICE CUSHING:

So then you say the question is really whether there is any rational basis for the prohibition. I assume that you disagree that the state has to show a compelling need for prohibition?

MR. PETERS:

That is correct, Your Honor. All that has to be shown is that the legislature acted rationally in saying to its citizens, "You shall not manufacture, sell, use, or possess this substance." There is also no requirement that the legislature ban everything that may be bad or harmful. The world is full of noxious substances—almost anything when used to excess can cause some degree of harm. But it is the function of the legislature, as representative of the people, and not of the courts, to make a determination of what should be prohibited. There is no doubt that the legislature could, if they wished, ban alcohol—in fact, some states to various extents do. They also have the constitutional power to ban tobacco or, if my opponent's description this morning was accurate, even tennis playing by, let's say, older people or people more likely to be subject to heart attacks.

MR. JUSTICE SPENCER:

How old would you say one would have to be
in order for him to be prohibited from playing
tennis?

MR. PETERS:

That would depend on the judgment of the legislature. I am not advocating prohibiting the playing
of tennis, Mr. Justice Spencer; I am just saying
that merely because a substance or activity may be
detrimental to some is not reason enough to require
that the legislature ban it before it may prohibit
something that is similarly harmful.

Certainly, tobacco could be constitutionally
banned. Pure nicotine is a deadly poison. It is rapidly absorbed through the skin, and a few drops
may be fatal. In fact, it has been used as an insecti-
cide, and during World War II, more tobacco was
used in the manufacture of nicotine-based insecti-
cides than was used for smoking. Furthermore,
while the other very real hazards of tobacco smoking are just now becoming known, many nations
have at one time or another in the past already
tried to prohibit its use. Spain and Japan in the
early seventeenth century restricted the cultivation
of tobacco, and in 1634, the czar of Russia forbade
smoking and decreed that anyone who was caught
smoking was to have his nose split. Recent scientific
evidence reveals that although their laws were
harsh, the instincts of these countries were correct.

There is no requirement, however, that tobacco
be banned before the use of heroin or marijuana
may be prohibited. It is sufficient that the legisla-

ture has made a rational decision that these substances are dangerous.

MR. JUSTICE PECKHAM:

You don't mean to imply that the dangers of marijuana and heroin are comparable, do you?

MR. PETERS:

I do not, Your Honor. My point is that there is no
requirement that the laws prohibiting the use or
sale of a substance be based on scientifically certain
evidence that the substance is more dangerous than
others that are not banned. Each prohibited item
has to be looked at on its own merits, and if there
is a rational basis for the prohibition, then the
prohibition is constitutional—except in those limited areas where an additional showing is necessary.
I would concede, for example, that the government
would have to demonstrate a compelling need before it could restrict the right of people to read
what they wished, because the right to receive and
transmit ideas is fully protected by specific guarantees in the First Amendment.

Now, counsel for Rodriguez has attempted to
demonstrate that marijuana is not as harmful as
many people think and may not, therefore, be
made illegal. I respectfully submit that there is
sufficient evidence to show that marijuana is not
as innocuous as he would have us think and that
there is a sufficient rational basis for its prohibition.

My opponent correctly noted that there are three
basic reasons why we believe that the commonwealth of Pennsylvania has acted rationally in prohibiting marijuana. First, we submit that there is

definite scientific evidence that marijuana can harm the individual user. Second, marijuana is clearly dangerous to society, and, third, there is substantial evidence that the use of marijuana, by some persons at least, encourages progression to the so-called hard narcotics like heroin or the extremely dangerous drugs like LSD. Any of these reasons would be sufficient to sustain Pennsylvania's prohibition of marijuana and to affirm Rodriguez' conviction.

First, let's see what marijuana does to the person who uses it. The following is a description of marijuana and its effects published by the President's Commission on Law Enforcement and the Administration of Justice in its Task Force Report on Narcotics and Drug Abuse:

> Its effects are rather complicated, combining both stimulation and depression. Much of its effect depends on the personality of the user. The drug may induce exaltation, joyousness and hilarity, and disconnected ideas; or it may induce quietude or reveries. In the inexperienced taker, it may induce panic. Or, one state may follow the other. Confused perceptions of space and time and hallucinations in sharp color may occur; the person's complex intellectual and motor functions may be impaired. These effects may follow within minutes of the time the drug is taken. The influence usually wears off within a few hours but may last much longer in the case of a

toxic dose. The immediate physical effects may
cause nausea and vomiting, but there are no
lasting physical effects and fatalities have not
been noted. Tolerance is very slight if it develops at all. Physical dependence does not
develop.

This description of marijuana was published in
1967, and while it is a good description of the effects that marijuana produces, I submit that its
implied conclusion that marijuana is not harmful
is in error. First of all, recent research conducted
under the auspices of the National Institute of
Mental Health has indicated, according to testimony given before a congressional subcommittee
in 1970 by the Institute's then director, Dr. Stanley
F. Yolles, that marijuana interferes with the thinking process and recent memory, that it weakens the
power to concentrate and subtly retards speech.
Drs. Zinberg and Weil, for example, have reported
that the person under the influence of marijuana
has extreme difficulty in remembering, from moment to moment, the logical thread of what he is
saying or thinking. This makes it extremely difficult for the person under the influence of marijuana to carry on a coherent conversation. In short,
marijuana is a mind-altering drug, and it adversely
affects the functioning of the human brain.

MR. JUSTICE CUSHING:
Don't we live in a society full of so-called mind-
altering drugs? We are all surrounded by depressants and stimulants, coffee can be addictive, and

even the cola drinks contain stimulants. People take all sorts of pills for everything today. What makes marijuana different? If it doesn't adversely affect the user beyond mere short-term feelings of euphoria, why shouldn't it be legalized?

MR. PETERS:

There is no doubt that people are using drugs as they never have before. Mind-altering substances, pep pills, depressants are all too common. Marijuana may not be too different in that respect. As I indicated earlier, each substance has to be looked at by itself. The question has to be asked whether this specific substance is or may be dangerous in and of itself—if it is, then there is a rational basis for the government to prohibit its use and, concomitantly, its manufacture and sale and possession.

It is clear, however, that marijuana is a substance that may indeed harm the user as well as society. The cola drinks, while they may be bad for the teeth, do not cause psychotic reactions—they do not render people incapable of thinking clearly or cloud their memories. Counsel for Rodriguez placed great emphasis on the LaGuardia committee's report and its supposed acquittal of marijuana. It is interesting that after all the facts were in, Mayor LaGuardia did not advocate legalizing marijuana. Evidently he found the report sufficiently disturbing, for he stated that it was not to be taken "as an encouragement" to indulgence.

Let's take a closer look at the report. In the preface to the clinical study, the researchers noted that toxic doses of marijuana have been known to produce psychotic reactions and that a study that had previously been done in New York City revealed marijuana users who had psychotic reactions to the drug. In some, the psychotic state continued for a number of days and hospitalization was required. To test this out, the researchers decided to administer the drug under controlled conditions. Out of the seventy-two subjects chosen for the experiment, nine suffered psychotic reactions induced by the drug.

MR. JUSTICE STANBERY:

Weren't the subjects chosen from the prison population in New York, and didn't they have histories of psychological problems?

MR. PETERS:

They did, but that doesn't make the statistics any less alarming. The experiment showed that marijuana can trigger psychotic episodes in people. It can release a whole horde of spirits lurking within each of us. The LaGuardia committee researchers concluded that "given the potential personality make-up and the right time and environment, marijuana may bring on a true psychotic state." This is the danger.

MR. JUSTICE BRADFORD:

Didn't the experiment conducted by Drs. Zinberg and Weil at the Boston University School of Medicine indicate that psychotic reactions were rare?

MR. PETERS:

That was their conclusion, Mr. Justice Bradford. But you will recall that they intended to test the effects of the drug with all of the variables removed.

Thus, the subjects were given the drug in a completely neutral and sterile environment, and more important, the subjects themselves were carefully screened to weed out any persons who might have had psychological problems. Now, while this experiment might have been a fair test to determine what marijuana—in and of itself—does to heartbeat or to the pupils, I submit that it was not a fair test to determine what effect marijuana will have upon the mental well-being of people generally. Most people suffer from some sort of mental problems that the use of marijuana could very well exacerbate.

Drs. Samuel Allentuck and Karl Bowman, who were part of the LaGuardia committee research team, have noted that although marijuana will not cause psychotic episodes in stable and well-integrated people, it can precipitate psychoses in people with unstable personalities. The doctors note that the marijuana psychosis is "protean in its manifestations" and may be mistaken for schizophrenic and other psychoneurotic or psychopathic reactions, and they state that psychotic reactions to marijuana could last for anywhere from a few hours to a few weeks. Similarly, one researcher at the Brooklyn State Hospital noted that of 114 patients who were admitted to the hospital in an eleven-month period for psychotic behavior, and who had a history of drug abuse, marijuana played what he called "an essential role" in symptomatology in nearly 8 percent and had precipitated schizophrenic episodes.

MR. JUSTICE STANBERY:

Isn't it possible that these patients were not normal before they used the drug?

MR. PETERS:

Of course it is. That is not my point. Even if we assume, for the sake of argument, that the conclusions of the researchers who hold that marijuana will not cause mental problems in psychologically normal persons when it is administered in the neutral environment of the laboratory are correct, still, I submit, that does not mean they can extrapolate the results from their clean experiments to the general population. Conditions in the laboratory are not the same as conditions in the real world. It makes as much sense for someone to assume that snow in the city will be as pristinely white as snow in the country as it does for one to assume that people in a real world under real conditions will be as unaffected by marijuana as people without psychological problems given controlled quantities of marijuana in a controlled environment. Significantly, Drs. Zinberg and Weil reported that all but one of the subjects who had never smoked marijuana before did not even get high in their experiment. Obviously, the drug is more potent under everyday conditions, or else it would not be so popular.

THE CHIEF JUSTICE:

Wasn't there evidence that only 50 percent of people who try the drug for the first time get high?

MR. PETERS:

Yes, but that may be because they don't know how

to smoke it. Marijuana smoke has to be inhaled into the lungs very deeply and kept there for a relatively long period of time or else it won't have much effect. But Drs. Zinberg and Weil carefully taught their subjects how to smoke, so this wasn't a factor.

Now, there is no doubt that marijuana can cause serious mental disturbances. Experiments conducted by Dr. Harris Isbell, a noted researcher in the field, demonstrate that marijuana, if taken in sufficient quantities, can produce a psychotic reaction in almost anyone. Reports from both India and Morocco, where use of the hemp plant as an intoxicant is particularly heavy, have stressed that excessive use can lead to severe mental problems that may be long-lasting. One researcher in India has noted that smoking cannabis so adversely affects the higher centers of the brain that if it is continued for a considerable length of time, it may lead even to insanity. In fact, one Moroccan survey notes that 25 percent of some 2,300 men admitted to psychiatric hospitals were diagnosed as suffering from cannabis psychoses.

Now, my adversary has stated many times that the fact that we haven't heard much about mental problems caused by marijuana on the college campuses is a reason to believe that everything is just fine. But this is not so. If the Court please, we are just beginning to get reports that marijuana can be very detrimental indeed to people's mental stability. Psychiatrists with our armed forces in Vietnam report that marijuana use over there has precipitated psychotic episodes in many GIs, and there have been reports from colleges and universities that—evidence to the contrary from the Princeton University study notwithstanding—marijuana use has not only adversely affected academic performance but has, in many instances, caused the student to lose all interest in schoolwork. Additionally, college health clinics report that many students who suffer from adverse psychological reactions to marijuana are now seeking aid. But these reports are only the tip of the iceberg. Marijuana is illegal, and many students do not seek medical aid for that reason, while others endure their frightful experiences aided by friends but without medical help.

Martin H. Keeler, while an associate professor at the University of North Carolina, published the results of interviews he had conducted with persons who suffered adverse mental reactions induced by marijuana. A large number of them suffered distinct paranoid reactions.

Let me note parenthetically that paranoia is one of the commonest mental reactions to marijuana. One of the earliest experimenters with marijuana in this country, Fitz Hugh Ludlow, noted in his diary, kept in the middle of the nineteenth century, that when he first tried the drug, "every moment increased the conviction that I was being watched. I did not know then, as I learned afterwards, that suspicion of all earthly things and persons was characteristic of the hasheesh delirium." Marijuana users commonly become paranoid

99

under its influence. Most often they are obsessed with the suspicion that the police are everywhere and that their closest friends are actually gendarmes in disguise. This reaction to marijuana is so prevalent that it even has a name and is called "fuzz fear."

To return to the Keeler interviews, let me cite his conclusions. Professor Keeler found that while marijuana may not be able to create what he called "functional psychopathology," it can precipitate this condition in individuals psychologically predisposed and that the use of marijuana "might precipitate trouble that would not have otherwise occurred." He also expressed the opinion that marijuana is potentially dangerous to people who have schizophrenic tendencies. Furthermore, Keeler reported, in work done with others, that marijuana use could trigger epileptic-type reactions and that its use by seizure-prone individuals was potentially dangerous.

If all this wasn't bad enough, we are now getting reports that adverse marijuana reactions, like adverse LSD reactions, may spontaneously recur; that is, a marijuana user who has suffered an adverse reaction while smoking might get another adverse reaction days or weeks later even though he hasn't smoked marijuana in the interval. This spontaneous recurrence effect is particularly dangerous because it can happen anywhere—even on the highway. But even more significantly, it means that the delicate chemical structure of the brain has been altered. People who use marijuana are clearly

playing a sort of chemical Russian roulette—no
one can be sure that severe psychological damage
won't be the result of marijuana use. As Dr. Stanley F. Yolles told the House of Representatives
Select Committee on Crime in October of 1969,
"There is reason to believe that the marijuana
user is exposed to an increased risk of either acute
or chronic psychologic damage each time he lights
a marijuana cigarette."

I respectfully submit that the evidence clearly
shows that marijuana can and does adversely affect
the mental health of many people. It is a definite
danger in this respect.

MR. JUSTICE BADGER:

If we assume that marijuana can trigger mental
problems in psychologically unstable people, why
should everyone be prohibited from using it?

MR. PETERS:

It is the judgment of the legislature that this
danger, even if only to some, warrants a general
prohibition. Just as everyone who may own bur-
glar's tools will not use them to steal, still the
threat of their illegal use is sufficient justification
for making their possession illegal. And so it is
with marijuana—its potential danger to susceptible
individuals in our society is a sufficient reason to
sustain its being made illegal for everyone.

My opponent's argument this morning, in which
he claimed that since we do not base censorship of
literature on the peculiarities of those who are
highly susceptible to erotic arousement, we cannot

therefore decide that a drug is harmful because of its potential adverse effects on certain people who are particularly disposed to psychological problems, is beside the point. Literature is specifically protected by the First Amendment, and the right of the majority to be free to read nonobscene literature transcends the right of the minority not to be exposed to material that they might subjectively think is obscene. Marijuana, however, is not specifically protected by the Constitution. While people have a fundamental human right to think or speak as they choose, they do not have a fundamental human right to act as they please. Just as my right to swing my arms stops short of my friend's nose, the right of people to use mind-altering substances freely must be conditioned on the rights of others who might be harmed. If there were a way to psychologically screen everyone who might use marijuana, to insure that they could not be adversely affected by the drug, then the answer might well be different. But there is no way to do this. Legalization of the drug is an all-or-nothing proposition. The so-called right to use marijuana must be qualified by, and subject to, the right of the government to protect those who would be harmed by it.

MR. JUSTICE BRADFORD:

I take it, then, that you reject John Stuart Mill's view that government has no business protecting the welfare of its citizens.

MR. PETERS:

I do, Your Honor. After all, government is merely

an extension of the individual—if I see a fellow human being about to harm himself, I have an obligation to try to stop him. So it is with government. This Court has consistently upheld legislation designed to protect the individual, despite the argument that everyone should fend for himself.

I am sure the argument was made many years ago when meat inspection laws were being considered that the government had no right to interfere with the business relationship between seller and consumer, and that if someone would be foolish enough to purchase tainted meat, then the purveyor should be permitted to sell it. That argument was without merit then and is without merit now. Not only does the government have the right, in appropriate circumstances, to protect people from their own folly or predispositions to self-destruction, but it has the obligation to do so.

It has been demonstrated with our little knowledge of the way marijuana acts that it can be dangerous to the mental stability of a significant number of people. That should be sufficient to sustain its prohibition.

MR. JUSTICE KING:

Is it relevant that the person whose mental condition might be most adversely affected by marijuana is the type of person who would be most likely to use it?

MR. PETERS:

It is highly relevant, Your Honor. It is precisely the type of person who is emotionally or mentally disturbed—and who will be most prone to psychotic illness—who will be most attracted to marijuana. Dr. Robert W. Baird, who is the founder and director of the Harlem H.A.V.E.N. clinic for narcotic addicts and who has had extensive experience with users of all kinds of drugs, testified before the House Select Committee on Crime in October of 1969 that anyone who smokes marijuana probably already has a mental problem.

There is a Moroccan saying that describes this phenomenon quite nicely; the Moroccan name for the intoxicating products of the *Cannabis* or hemp plant is "kif," and the saying goes: "You are a kif addict long before you smoke your first pipe."

The fact that people who are unusually subject to psychological problems are attracted to marijuana makes it especially dangerous. Dr. Zinberg admits that people who are emotionally or psychologically disturbed may be adversely affected by the drug, and Dr. Yolles has reported to Congress that marijuana can trigger acute panic, depression, and psychotic reactions. It is precisely the people who are most attracted to marijuana who must be protected from their own self-destructive tendencies, and we believe that this is sufficient reason for its continued prohibition.

MR. JUSTICE BRADFORD:
You are not saying that everyone who uses marijuana is mentally disturbed or even that every mentally disturbed person who uses marijuana gets psychotic reactions, are you?

MR. PETERS:
Absolutes are impossible to defend. No, Your

Honor, I am not saying that everyone with mental problems will be adversely affected by marijuana— I am just saying that there is an increased risk of psychological damage and that this increased risk warrants continued suppression of the drug. Not only don't we know the extent of marijuana's effect on the mentally disturbed person, but we don't know how the drug may subtly affect the mentally stable person. Much more research will have to be done before we will know any definite answers. In the meantime, the drug should not be turned loose.

Mr. Justice Woodward:

It seems to me that much of the controversy over marijuana and its alleged effects stems from the fact that people aren't really talking about the same thing when they discuss its dangers. It was mentioned earlier this morning that the products of the hemp plant vary enormously in potency— that, for instance, hashish is up to six times as potent as the marijuana commonly smoked in this country and that the marijuana grown in Mexico is more potent than the homegrown variety. Why can't marijuana be regulated the same way alcohol is regulated, as to both consistency and strength, so that the more dangerous and potent products of the hemp plant can be retained in the illegal category while a standardized less potent marijuana can be legalized?

Mr. Peters:

Like the near-beer of the 1920s?

Mr. Justice Woodward:

Perhaps.

MR. PETERS:

It might be something for the legislature to consider when we learn more about marijuana and its effects. Right now, we know almost nothing about how it affects the body. Perhaps someday, when all the returns are in, the legislature will decide to legalize marijuana and regulate it as you suggest—but we simply do not know enough now. What we do know, however, gives us sufficient reason to keep marijuana illegal, and certainly the laws prohibiting marijuana are not constitutionally invalid.

THE CHIEF JUSTICE:

Mr. Peters, how do you respond to Mr. Smith's contention that marijuana does not cause crime?

MR. PETERS:

I will admit that most research groups like the LaGuardia committee and studies like that issued by the President's Commission on Law Enforcement and the Administration of Justice have reported that marijuana, in and of itself, does not cause crime the way a flame can cause fire. But marijuana does have other effects that may indirectly, if not cause crime, lead to antisocial behavior. While it is not a controlling factor in the commission of crimes, marijuana may very well be a contributing factor because it tends to lower the inhibitions of the user. Dr. Walter Bromberg, whose report Mr. Justice Woodward referred to earlier, explains this point. Dr. Bromberg, who, in addition to having been the senior psychiatrist at New York's Bellevue Hospital, was for many years chief psychiatrist in New York City's criminal courts, noted that marijuana can "breed" crime when used by psychopathic types because it allows the emergence of aggressive, sexual, or antisocial tendencies. A study conducted in Morocco indicated that many violent crimes were committed by persons who were under the influence of cannabis at the time.

It seems clear that persons with criminal tendencies may be less able to suppress them while under the influence of marijuana. In this respect, marijuana may act somewhat like alcohol, although I can't cite statistics comparable to those which my opponent gave you with regard to the number of people who committed various crimes while under the influence of alcohol.

MR. JUSTICE STANBERY:

How do you account for your inability to do so?

MR. PETERS:

First of all, as my adversary noted earlier, there is no reliable method of detecting marijuana in the body. Thus, the police may not be aware that a suspect arrested immediately after a crime has been using marijuana. This is in contrast to the situation that exists with alcohol, for a person under the influence of liquor is easy to spot. Secondly, many criminals, if indeed they are apprehended, are arrested only long after the crime has been committed, so there is no opportunity to check for a relationship between that crime and marijuana. Thirdly, and perhaps most importantly, marijuana, despite its recent popularity, is still not used nearly to the extent that alcohol is, and therefore we don't know what its effect on the suppressed criminal tendencies of the population at large might be.

In any event, neither alcohol nor marijuana will inevitably cause crime or antisocial behavior in normal individuals. Many people get drunk and do nothing more than fall asleep. Now, while it is true that marijuana may tend to make many people contemplative and quiet, this reaction, as researchers have noted, is largely dependent upon the environment in which the drug is taken and the individual disposition of the user. Thus, as I've noted, many users suffer paranoid reactions while under the influence of marijuana. They may suspect that people are about to do them in and may strike out in a mistaken attempt at self-defense. One young marijuana user testified before the House Select Committee on Crime in 1969 that he blanked out and tried to stab his brother while he was under the influence of marijuana. Just as liquor can be drunk at the normal social cocktail party with no adverse consequences but can also be the precipitating factor for violence when used, let's say, by a motorcycle gang on a weekend spree, marijuana also has varied effects on the user. As Drs. Allentuck and Bowman, who were part of the LaGuardia committee research team, noted, marijuana, like alcohol, does not alter the basic personality of the user, but it can, by relaxing inhibitions, release antisocial tendencies formerly suppressed. As Dr. Yolles said, in testifying before the House Select Committee on Crime, while people under the influence of marijuana tend to be passive, crimes are committed by persons under its influence as they are by people who are under the influence of any drug that loosens self-control.

Dr. Victor Vogel of the California Rehabilitation Center has compiled experiences of some one hundred heroin addicts while they were using just marijuana. One noted that "I got in quite a bit of trouble while I was high on marijuana—steal to get money to party and to buy marijuana; got involved in gang fights and was arrested twice for rape." Another stated, "Under the influence of marijuana, I broke into a church and robbed the collection box." A third said that marijuana makes him paranoid and that, as a result, he gets into fights. A fourth told how he burglarized fifteen drugstores searching for narcotics and how he used to get high on marijuana before attempting the burglaries. Another told how he and a friend, both high on marijuana, were walking down a street when his friend for no reason at all began to beat a passerby. Still another commented about marijuana's effect upon him in this way: "I have gotten into plenty of trouble while high on marijuana, gang fights, and I beat up my wife."

MR. JUSTICE STANBERY:

How reliable are these statements? We know nothing about the individual tendencies of the people involved. They might have been antisocial without having used marijuana. They might be blaming marijuana for their own inadequacies.

MR. PETERS:

That's true, Your Honor. But I think the point they make is that marijuana can influence behavior. That is all I am suggesting. It can adversely affect young people, unlike water, for example, or cherry soda. No matter how antisocial a person may be, I don't think you will find him bolstering his courage with water or beating his wife after gulping down a pitcher of cherry soda.

No—marijuana is a mind-altering drug. It affects people's way of looking at the world. It can bring out demons long suppressed. That is the danger as I see it. It is interesting to note that when a person has lost his head and has perpetrated some violent act, we say that he has "run amuck." In the Malayan language "amuck" and "cannabis" are synonyms.

Now, despite protestations to the contrary by my adversary and some researchers, there is evidence that marijuana definitely tends to release sexual inhibitions. Studies in India show that cannabis is commonly used as an aphrodisiac, and one study of chronic cannabis users in that country reveals that over 10 percent first tried the drug in order to increase their sexual prowess and pleasures. In this country, there is repeated evidence that marijuana is also used as an adjunct to increased sexual activity. One twenty-two-year-old college senior, who later went on to graduate school in business, reported marijuana's effect this way:

> Once you get the idea into your head that you want to get your hands on her, there's very little that can stop you. And you don't care. . . . Sex is a more purely physical high,

that's the only problem. It's a lust orgy. When you are involved in it, you don't think about the girl at all, you just think about the physical pleasure. But the physical pleasure is just immense. . . . Marijuana acts as a frighteningly powerful aphrodisiac.

One eighteen-year-old college girl stated that "pot makes you a sex fiend. You don't necessarily want sex more, but you enjoy it more." Studies of marijuana users in the Army have similarly shown that the drug creates a lust for sex and can lead to sexual perversions. One soldier told an interviewer that "after you smoke it you feel that no woman can resist you." One 1946 study of marijuana users in the Army noted that many of the men who were interviewed "frankly admitted that only when under the influence of marijuana were they able to enjoy homosexual and perverted behavior. The sense of shame and disgust disappears under marijuana to be replaced by the overpowering desire for sexual gratification at the level of infantile behavior." Parties were described where "everything went" and the participants were without a sense of shame and eagerly regressed "to a childish level of sensuality" where accepted standards of morality were flouted. The men reported that when under the influence of marijuana they vied with each other to see who could perform the most disgusting act.

Now, I am not saying that marijuana will cause everyone to behave in this manner. Of course it won't. I'm just saying that by lowering the inhibitions, marijuana can permit people to do horrible things—both to their detriment and to the detriment of society. My point is that, at the present time, we simply do not know what effect marijuana will have on suppressed antisocial tendencies of the public generally if its use is suddenly made legal. We have been fortunate so far, because marijuana is not legal. Thus, most people have not been exposed to it—and the others cannot get all they may desire. Legalization will only open the floodgates.

Now, much has been said this morning to the effect that marijuana is not physically dangerous. However, we know next to nothing about marijuana's effect on the human body, and what we do know indicates that it might be very dangerous.

MR. JUSTICE STANBERY:
Haven't studies of long-term chronic users indicated that marijuana does not harm the body? And didn't the report of the President's Commission on Law Enforcement and the Administration of Justice, in that excerpt which you read to us earlier, indicate that there were no lasting physical effects of marijuana use?

MR. PETERS:
That's correct, Your Honor. But merely because some adverse effects have not yet become apparent doesn't mean that the substance is physically harmless. It has taken a long time for the true physical effects of tobacco to become known, and they are not fully understood even today. Par-

enthetically, I for one can't see how inhaling marijuana smoke deep into the lungs and holding it there for about twenty seconds cannot severely damage their delicate mechanisms. In any event, this potential danger is currently being studied. More frightening, however, are some recent reports that marijuana, like LSD, may be teratogenic, that is it may cause women to give birth to deformed babies. Now, while there is no evidence yet that this can happen in the human being, several experimenters have shown that marijuana does cause deformed young in hamsters, rabbits, and rats. Until more research is done, this fact alone should militate against legalizing marijuana.

Other recent studies have also indicated that marijuana may not be as innocuous as some would like to believe. It has been shown, for example, that THC, the active chemical in the hemp resin that gives marijuana its mind-altering properties, inhibits some of the metabolic enzymes in the liver. Briefly, the liver breaks down toxic materials and is, in a sense, nature's purification plant for the body. Interfering with its action could be very harmful indeed. There is already some evidence that a liver that has metabolized THC cannot effectively metabolize a number of other drugs—such as barbiturates—and that subsequent ingestion of these other drugs may be very dangerous and possibly fatal. It is also interesting that in India, Egypt, and Morocco, where cannabis is widely used, there are numerous reports of extensive physical damage caused by the drug. The fact of the matter is that we simply do not know what adverse effects marijuana may have on the body, and we won't know until more research is done.

Although research hasn't yet indicated the true extent of the dangers of marijuana-triggered psychoses or the nature of its adverse effect upon the physical well-being of the body, marijuana is dangerous for yet another reason—it camouflages people's emotional problems. There is a great deal of evidence that some people use marijuana, as others use alcohol, as a means of escaping from the miseries of their everyday lives. This is especially true in India and Africa, where use is particularly heavy. The LaGuardia report noted, and other studies have confirmed, that marijuana induces, as part of its euphoria, a sense of well-being and satisfaction. It is thus particularly attractive to those among us who have difficulty coping with the problems of life. It is also highly attractive to youngsters for this reason.

Adolescence is a very difficult time. The so-called growing pains are not only physical aches that result from the growing of our bodies, but mental disturbances that result from the growing of our minds. Realization that the world is not a warm comfortable womb is a severe shock to most young people. They find it hard to understand the complexities and, yes, the hypocrisies of the real world. Reactions among youngsters are different. Some accept the challenge and are prepared to conquer the world on its own terms. They will join society and compete for the goods, both physical and emotional, that society has to offer. They will fit in, and will lead useful lives. Others, on the other hand—and unfortunately this group is growing—will not enter into the mainstream of societal life. Upon emerging from their sheltered nests, they will see the shadows of their own inadequacies, real or imagined, against the background of an often cruel and impersonal world. Frightened, they will retreat to the comfortable safety of their own little worlds. These worlds are too often the universities, which have, of late, been taking on the characteristics of little cloistered ecological units, each a self-sustaining and self-perpetuating pocket of freedom from the turmoil found in the real world.

Marijuana is the perfect drug for people who cannot cope with the world and its problems. It gives them feelings of adequacy and increases their self-confidence and self-esteem. But, contrary to popular folklore, marijuana use does not heighten creativity, it only gives the user the illusion of creativity. It leads him to think that his music is sweeter or his paintings are more relevant. It also turns his thoughts inward and makes him introspective. Indeed, the introspection that marijuana produces is just the type of mental masturbation that gives the marijuana user the illusion of intellectualism and of self-realization.

Marijuana is, in short, a cruel hoax. While creating a veneer of intellectual fertility, it makes true accomplishment more difficult. Alexander the Great, the most powerful man of his time, once demanded that his teacher Aristotle give him some secret so he could learn without having to study. Aristotle replied that there was no royal road to knowledge. Similarly, there is no royal road to increased creativity or insight.

A University of California researcher conducted a little experiment on three students who claimed that marijuana gave them great insight and heightened their creative processes. He tape-recorded their comments while they were under the influence of marijuana. After the effects of the drug wore off, he replayed what they had said. He reports that they were so appalled at the verbal drivel being played back to them that they wept.

This shock at discovering that the so-called royal road leads not to Nirvana but to the garbage dump is not new. Dr. Oliver Wendell Holmes, the father of the late Supreme Court Justice of the same name, wrote of a somewhat similar experience. One day he went to the dentist to have a tooth extracted and was given nitrous oxide, or laughing gas, as an anesthetic. Holmes' experience under the influence of this drug was so powerful that, when he awoke, he was convinced that he had discovered the golden key to eternal truth. Wanting to recapture this holy vision, he persuaded his dentist to put him under the gas once again. As he was going under, he asked for a pencil, and in the height of serene communion with the forces of the universe, he hastily scribbled a few precious words. When he awoke, he anxiously asked to see what he had written. The words were: "Lord, what a stench!"

The late George Orwell once related a similar story to Arthur Koestler, who tells it this way: "A friend of his, while living in the Far East, smoked several pipes of opium every night, and every night a single phrase rang in his ear, which contained the whole secret of the universe; but in his euphoria he could not be bothered to write it down and by the morning it was gone. One night he managed to jot down the magic phrase after all, and in the morning he read: 'The banana is big, but its skin is even bigger.'"

No, marijuana, or any other drug, cannot provide the toll for any "royal road"; it can only give the addict the illusion of increased awareness, and he will develop a reliance on synthetic experiences. The marijuana addict not only has his vision of the world distorted but develops a habit of escaping from all unpleasantness and all discomfort.

MR. JUSTICE WOODWARD:
Addict? I thought it was agreed that marijuana is not addictive.

MR. PETERS:
Excuse me, Your Honor, I misspoke. I meant that the chronic user of marijuana develops the habit of escaping from all unpleasantness and all discomfort and thus sits on the sidelines of life, occasionally watching and criticizing the game being played in the real world by real people.

As long as the subject has been brought up, however, let me explain marijuana habituation. It is true that marijuana is not physically addictive in the sense in which that term is generally understood. A chronic user of marijuana who stops taking the drug will not experience the symptoms of a physical withdrawal as will, let's say, the user of heroin. The heroin addict will suffer intense muscle aches, cramps, and nausea against a background of severe depression. Marijuana does not produce these effects. Neither does cocaine, for that matter. However, marijuana, like cocaine, is psychologically addictive. For example, chronic users who have suddenly had their supply cut off have demonstrated anxiety, restlessness, and irritability.

MR. JUSTICE BADGER:

The same symptoms we see in someone who has given up tobacco?

MR. PETERS:

Marijuana develops a greater psychological dependence than tobacco, Your Honor. Not smoking tobacco can be very unpleasant to the chronic smoker. The cessation of marijuana smoking by a chronic user deprives him of a mental crutch, something that helps him cope with the unfriendly real world. As one young person responded when asked how frequently he used the drug, "Pot? It's my life!" Another, paraphrasing an orange juice commercial on television, noted that "a day without marijuana is like a day without sunshine."

Now, not every person who tries marijuana will develop this psychological dependence. Certainly, many young people will try marijuana once or twice and then give it up. But Dr. Yolles estimates that 10 percent of all those who try marijuana become chronic users or so-called "pot-heads." These pot-heads will spend the major portion of their time and energy in getting and using the drug. They withdraw from the reality of life, lose ambition and drive, and generally fade into the shadows of life, bemused by the images which marijuana produces.

This 10-percent figure is highly significant. It is estimated that only about 7 percent of this nation's ninety-three million adults who have tried alcohol become alcoholics or heavy drinkers.

MR. JUSTICE PECKHAM:

How reliable is that 10-percent figure? Doesn't the fact that marijuana is illegal mean that people who use it and become chronic users are not representative samples of the population as a whole?

MR. PETERS:

That's true, Your Honor—but when you consider that marijuana is harder to obtain than alcohol, the 10-percent figure might indeed be low. If marijuana were more readily available, more people would be able to become chronic users.

MR. JUSTICE SPENCER:

Well, doesn't it come down to the fact that this is a drug-oriented culture and that people, all people, not just marijuana users, take pills and liquor to escape from the rigors of everyday life?

MR. PETERS:

I agree that we are now living in or are on the verge of a drug culture. There is a growing inability of people to cope with life and an increasing desire to escape from it. But this doesn't mean that we should add a new drug to the list. The psychiatrists are fighting a holding battle as it is—

we should not add to their task. The solution to the problems of society is not to provide a new vehicle for escape but to repair those features that need fixing. Legalizing marijuana will not solve anything, it will just make people oblivious to real problems, which will then never get solved.

The habit of escape is very harmful to the individual user. As noted earlier this morning by one of the Justices—I believe it was Mr. Justice Bradford—the human being must learn to cope with the realities of life if he is to mature and develop normally. The adolescent who uses marijuana will learn too early in life to take the easy way out. This was emphasized by Dr. Yolles in testimony before the House Select Committee on Crime in October of 1969 when he expressed concern over the effect of continued use of what he called "a reality-distorting agent" on the future psychological development of the adolescent user. He pointed out that adolescence is a time of great psychological turmoil and that the patterns of coping with reality are developed during this period and play a significant role in the behavior of the future adult. He warned that "persistent use of an agent which serves to ward off reality during this critical developmental period is likely to compromise seriously the future ability of the individual to make an adequate adjustment to a complex society."

MR. JUSTICE KING:
That's all well and good—but aren't you really setting up a straw man? I think your opponent was

in agreement that just as alcohol may be harmful
to the young person so may marijuana, and that
if marijuana is legalized, it should be restricted to
adult use—just as alcohol is today.

MR. PETERS:

I have no quarrel with that, Your Honor—but
there also are many adults whom marijuana might
harm, whose ability to cope with society would be
lessened if marijuana were legalized. It has been
shown, for example, that regular use of marijuana
contributes to apathy, loss of effectiveness, and inability to carry out long-term plans. Marijuana
users are forever dreaming up great schemes—to
be accomplished tomorrow. Additionally, chronic
users of marijuana cannot endure frustration and
cannot concentrate effectively. In sum, they remove
themselves from the mainstream of society: to use
a popular term, they drop out.

MR. JUSTICE BADGER:

Isn't it one of the basic tenets of civilization that
adults should be given the opportunity to decide
for themselves whether they will cope with society
or just drop out? If they want to drop out, then
isn't it their right to do so? In any event, what
evidence is there that marijuana will lessen their
ability—as opposed to the ability of adolescents—to
cope with society?

MR. PETERS:

Well, people may have a theoretical right to drop
out of society, but I don't think that society has any
right to encourage them to do so, if only for its
own preservation. Legalizing marijuana will be

just such an encouragement. It has been clearly shown that where there is widespread use of marijuana among the adult population, people become less productive; they lose their incentive and just drift off into a corner of their drug-created world. India and Morocco have their hashish skid rows just as we have our alcoholic skid rows.

MR. JUSTICE BRADFORD:

I thought that hashish was more potent than the variety of marijuana commonly smoked here.

MR. PETERS:

It is, Mr. Justice Bradford.

MR. JUSTICE BRADFORD:

Then how relevant is it to speak of a loss of productivity among people in countries where hashish is smoked rather than marijuana?

MR. PETERS:

It is relevant because that is the only experience we have with widespread use of the drug. Limited experience here in this country confirms that marijuana will produce similar results.

MR. JUSTICE BRADFORD:

Aren't there numerous reports that professional people and others who are regularly employed also smoke marijuana and do not fade into the shadows?

MR. PETERS:

Yes, Your Honor. Just as people can use alcohol without winding up in a flophouse, so too I guess people can use marijuana and continue their involvement in society. But the potential for misuse is there. For example, it has been shown in this country that the regular use of marijuana has severe detrimental effects. Highly instructive is the description given by the LaGuardia committee researchers of a tea pad party that they gave for their subjects in order to observe what effects marijuana would have in an environment closely duplicating the setting in which it was frequently smoked. The men were given as many marijuana cigarettes as they wanted. The researchers reported that when the cigarettes were distributed, the subjects crowded around with their hands outstretched, like children begging for candy. The group broke up into cells of two or three to do their smoking. The researchers reported that the men would laugh and joke and would get into discussions and arguments that never seemed to get anywhere, and that illogical reasoning was never recognized by the persons to whom it was addressed. Gradually, the subjects gathered around the radio and listened to the music, slowly swaying in their chairs. The researchers reported that, in general, the smokers conveyed the impression of being adolescents. As the report noted—and now I'm quoting—"One forgot that they were actually adults with all the usual adult responsibilities. One could not help drawing the conclusion that they, too, had forgotten it for the time being." Now, while it is true that these men did not have the highest IQ in the world, they were of normal intelligence, with an average IQ of 99, the range extending from 70 to 124. And while they came from the lower socioeconomic levels of society and were drawn from New York City's prisons, they were certainly representative of at least some sections of our society.

Dr. Robert Baird similarly reports that the person who resorts to marijuana to escape from troubles will become emotionally immature, introverted, and selfish. As Dr. Baird has noted, if marijuana were ever legalized or the penalties were lessened, this nation would lose "a generation of young, productive people who would become destroyed by the hedonistic, pleasure-seeking syndrome of getting high." In light of what we now know—based on the limited amount of research that has been done so far—I am at a loss to see how anyone can advocate turning loose such a potentially socially debilitating drug upon a largely unsuspecting society.

Now, not only does marijuana psychologically harm the individual by giving him a convenient vehicle in which to escape from the cares of the real world, but it also gets him into the habit of using drugs. At first, the person will use marijuana because his friends will tell him it's fun or good or because he is just curious to see what the fuss is all about. He tries it a few times, and perhaps he doesn't get any reaction because he doesn't know how to smoke it properly. Someone will show him the correct way of dragging on a reefer, or perhaps he discovers the proper method by himself and he enjoys the sensations. He feels free and relaxed. If he likes art, he may find that paintings seem more intense; the sensations of color may seem heightened. If he enjoys music, it will seem richer, more sensuous. He finds that marijuana doesn't dull his sensations as does alcohol, but sharpens them. Equally important, he finds that marijuana, unlike alcohol, will not give him a hangover. It seems to give him a whole new perspective on the world—things seem to fall into coherent patterns. At last, he can recognize the world for all its hypocrisy. He feels good. The drug has armed him with a feeling of self-confidence and self-esteem. He feels as though there isn't anything he can't do if he wished.

For a while, the person will take marijuana only to relax and enjoy external stimulation such as art, music, or sex. He has discovered the perfect drug, or so he thinks. It produces pleasure without pain, is much more convenient to carry than alcohol, and is about as inexpensive. Then one day he gets into a depressed mood—things aren't going too well at the office or school, his wife or girl friend is giving him trouble, or what have you. He remembers how good marijuana made him feel. Perhaps it can snap him out of his depression. He gives it a try. It works. He feels great. He is relaxed again, euphoria has drowned out his depression, and he has lost the self-doubts that had been haunting him a bit earlier. Everything is just fine. Now he uses marijuana not only to relax but also to pull himself out of those minor depressions in which we all find ourselves sometimes. He really feels great. He does his work better and is at peace with the world because he knows he can always regain that extra spark of life by just lighting up and drifting back into a miasma of marijuana smoke, riding the magic carpet to Nirvana.

Then one day his depression is a little worse, a little deeper than it has been before, and marijuana doesn't work quite so well. In fact, it may even produce some adverse reactions. It may heighten his anxiety and make him nervous. Hallucinations may frighten him, and he may be plunged into the depths of paranoia. Then a friend may describe a recent trip on LSD or describe the magical effects of cocaine or opium or heroin. He knows how good he once felt using marijuana, so perhaps these new drugs will be just the thing. In any event, because he has a new depression that he can't handle, or because he is seeking an even greater kick, he will try the hard and concededly dangerous drugs. He is now hooked, and it won't be long before he is supporting a habit that costs from twenty-five to two hundred dollars a day or before his brains become like loosely scrambled eggs.

MR. JUSTICE BRADFORD:
I thought there was scientific proof that marijuana use will not lead to addiction to hard narcotics. Didn't your opponent say that Dr. Yolles estimates that less than 5 percent of chronic marijuana users go on to heroin?

MR. PETERS:
He did, Your Honor. Let me answer your question this way. It is true—at least all the scientific studies say so—that there is nothing in the physical properties of marijuana that will lead to heroin addic-

tion in the same inevitable way that eating a lot of salt or a pizza pie will make you thirsty. I'll concede that; my point is that using marijuana makes one more predisposed to taking other drugs. It in effect opens the door. The marijuana smoker will recall how he didn't crumble to dust when he took his first drag on a marijuana cigarette. In fact, he remembers how nice it made him feel—if he did it correctly. He becomes used to taking drugs to feel good, to escape, to relax, or what have you. It is a very simple and short step from using marijuana like everyone else to using LSD or methedrine or heroin like everyone else.

Now, Dr. Yolles does estimate that less than 5 percent of the chronic marijuana users go on to heroin. I don't know how he gets that figure, but anyway he seems to confine himself to heroin, and I'd be interested in learning how many chronic marijuana users go on to the other dangerous drugs when they find that marijuana is not quite strong enough to drag them out of their misery or to propel them on a trip quite as far out as they would like. A study conducted at the Federal Narcotics Treatment Center in Lexington, Kentucky, showed that 80 percent of the heroin addicts had a history of marijuana use. Dr. James L. Goddard, former director of the U.S. Food and Drug Administration, estimates that marijuana has been the drug first used by 90 to 95 percent of heroin addicts.

MR. JUSTICE BADGER:
Didn't Dr. Goddard once say that marijuana was less dangerous than alcohol?

MR. PETERS:

I think he said that the *known* dangers of marijuana may be less than those of alcohol. In 1967 he was misquoted by the press as saying that he would rather his daughter smoked marijuana than drank liquor. Although he strenuously denied making that statement, and even received an apology from the wire service that put the story out, it was widely circulated. In fact, someone at the Department of Health, Education, and Welfare circulated the following limerick:

> A well-known physician named Jim,
> Has really gone out on a limb.
> Believe it or not,
> He decided that pot
> Is better than drinking straight gin.

Actually Dr. Goddard emphasized that he would object to his daughter's trying marijuana because it is dangerous to drive under its influence and we don't know enough about its long-term effects, such as possible damage to the chromosomes. As I noted earlier, recent research indicates that marijuana can cause malformations in the offspring of some animals.

In any event there is strong evidence that the use of marijuana makes it easier for people to progress to the hard drugs. People who have to live with the problem report that there is a direct relationship between the use of marijuana and progression to the hard drugs. Dr. Robert Baird, who is, as I noted earlier, the founder and director of the H.A.V.E.N. Drug Clinic in Harlem and is a renowned expert in this field, testified before the House Select Committee on Crime in October of 1969 as to his personal observations of the way marijuana affects people. I wish the Court would read his entire testimony because it eloquently portrays the very real danger of progression from marijuana to the hard drugs. He testified that he had been working with drug addicts in Harlem since 1950 and has seen addiction or habituation to all sorts of drugs. Dr. Baird contends that marijuana is a very dangerous drug, and he has severely criticized other doctors, including Dr. Yolles, who have advocated reducing the penalty for possession.

Let me say at this point that neither Dr. Yolles nor any other responsible government official or physician recommends legalizing marijuana, because, as we also contend, there is not enough known about marijuana to loose it upon the general public.

Dr. Baird testified that he had worked with close to a thousand addicts and that 95 percent of them had started with marijuana. He brought seven of them to the committee and let them explain their story. They all started on marijuana and went on to experiment with other drugs. One of them, a young man who had started to smoke while he was in the Army and stationed in Korea, testified that he had smoked marijuana for a while and then went on to opium. He tried it out of curiosity. Finally, he went to heroin, and he blames it all on marijuana. He eloquently testified as to the danger of legalizing marijuana. Let me just quote part of his testimony.

Now people, if they cut grass loose to the public it would be an unbelievable thing that would happen, because by making grass legal, this would give people a greater—like they would want to know what something else was like. You would get people that never touched anything at all and all of a sudden grass would come on the market, you can buy a package of grass, twenty cigarettes for say a quarter, a half dollar or a dollar, or whatever it would be and they would get high off grass. These are people who never touched anything before, maybe took a few drinks or got drunk once in a while. Now, by smoking grass they would know what it is to be high, they hear about somebody else who had hash and they say to them hash is a concentrated grass and you get much higher. So they would go to hash, and from hash they would go on and on and on until they really just ruined their life.

Another boy testified how he and his friend started on marijuana in high school and how after a while, after they went to college, marijuana wouldn't do anything for them anymore so they started on heroin.

Now, while it may be true that a person who goes on to heroin from marijuana may be predisposed to such progression, I say that marijuana gives them part if not all of that predisposition. It gets them into the habit of seeking relief from drugs. In February of 1970, Jackie Robinson, the former great Brooklyn Dodger ballplayer, testified before a Maryland commission looking into the dangers of narcotic addiction. He lashed out at what he termed "experts" who say marijuana is not harmful, noting how his son had started smoking marijuana when he was in the Army in Vietnam and had progressed to heroin when he returned home. Robinson's son told him that "only the strong can truly smoke marijuana and not go the next step."

Dr. Baird has predicted that if marijuana is legalized, there will be between half a million and a million heroin addicts by 1975. I think the evidence is clear that legalization of marijuana will open the floodgates to the increased use of other dangerous drugs, including heroin. This danger alone, we submit, provides a sufficient basis for sustaining the laws under challenge today.

MR. JUSTICE WOODWARD:
Weren't Dr. Baird and the others talking about young people—that marijuana will lead young people on to heroin and the other so-called hard drugs? Can't the sale of marijuana, if it is legalized, be restricted to adults, just as the sale of alcohol is restricted to adults?

MR. PETERS:
Legalization will put the stamp of acceptability on

marijuana, and it will be very easy for young people to get it.

MR. JUSTICE WOODWARD:

Can't they get it now if they want to, even though it is illegal?

MR. PETERS:

I respectfully submit that that is no reason to legalize it—you don't spray your house with a flamethrower merely because part of it happens to be on fire. The problem of marijuana use by youngsters will not be solved by restricting its sale to adults. Adults, too, seeking greater kicks, will progress to the more potent and dangerous drugs. No, there is a very great drug problem. The legalization of marijuana will not solve anything, it will only make things worse.

There is still another reason why we feel that laws prohibiting the possession of marijuana are a reasonable exercise of the states' power to protect their citizens. There is no doubt that it is dangerous to drive under the influence of marijuana just as it is dangerous to drive under the influence of alcohol or any drug that slows the reflexes and alters normal perception. Now, earlier this morning, my adversary discussed, at seeming great length, an experiment conducted at the Division of Research of the Department of Motor Vehicles at Olympia, Washington. He stated that this experiment, conducted in the laboratory under sterile conditions, tended to prove that marijuana affected driving skills less than alcohol. This may be true, although the experiment was criticized by Dr. Sidney Cohen, director of the Division of Narcotic Addiction and Drug Abuse of the National Institute of Mental Health, before the House Select Committee on Crime in October of 1969. Dr. Cohen pointed out that although large doses of alcohol were administered to the subjects, the amount of marijuana given was unknown because the cigarettes were not properly analyzed.

In any event, it is dangerous to drive under the influence of marijuana because it distorts the user's perception of time and space. Briefly what this means is that the driver under the influence of marijuana will not realize how fast he is going, how far he has traveled, or just how far he is from the other cars on the highway. These distortions —even if we accept the testimony that reflex actions are unimpaired—make the marijuana-intoxicated driver exceedingly dangerous. Just how dangerous can be seen from the following statement by a twenty-eight-year-old physician:

I often drive my automobile when I'm high on marijuana and have never had any actual problems doing so. But I do have some purely subjective difficulty. . . . My reflexes and perception seem to be O.K. but I have problems like this: I'll come to a stop light and have a moment of panic because I can't remember whether or not I've just put my foot on the brake. Of course, when I look down it's there, but in the second or two afterwards I can't remember having done it. In a similar way,

I can't recall whether I've passed a turn I want
to take, or even whether I've made the turn.

What makes this statement especially frightening is that one gets the impression that the young
man in question doesn't consider driving while
intoxicated on marijuana to be dangerous. It's that
strange feeling of invincibility that marijuana users
seem to have. People under the influence of marijuana just can't perceive objects accurately; things
close seem to be far away, and vice versa. Feelings
of invincibility may prompt some to attempt to
drive between two oncoming headlights, or to drive
under a huge truck.

MR. JUSTICE STANBERY:
Why can't we protect ourselves from a person who
drives under the influence of marijuana just as we
protect ourselves from the drunk driver—by the
imposition of criminal penalties?

MR. PETERS:
With twenty to thirty thousand deaths each year
traceable to drunk driving, it seems that we don't
protect ourselves too well from those who drive
under the influence of alcohol. But even strict enforcement of driving regulations would be insufficient. It is easy to determine if a person is under
the influence of alcohol. The level of alcohol intoxication may be accurately measured by a variety of
inexpensive devices. However, there is no easy or
even reliable method of determining whether someone is under the influence of marijuana. It would
thus be impossible to enforce laws against driving

while under its influence. Forbidding its possession and use is therefore the only practical method
of preventing people from driving while intoxicated
by marijuana.

There is still another reason why the laws banning marijuana should be sustained. As I noted
earlier, legalization of marijuana would carry with
it the very real danger of producing a nation of
drug-dependent, listless, driveless automatons. One
of the foremost rights of society is the right of
self-protection. Society has the absolute right to
protect itself from destruction by enemies within,
as well as without, and the laws against marijuana
serve to protect society from a subtly dangerous
drug that alters and redirects human energies inward. We must not permit an overly theoretical
view of liberality to destroy our society by per-
suading us to so alter its laws that we ingrain and
condone the habit of escaping all unpleasantness
and discomfort by resort to drugs. We must not
let our civilization turn into a disunified mass of
valueless individuals who have sidestepped life. I
respectfully suggest that legalization of marijuana
will do precisely that.

THE CHIEF JUSTICE:
Mr. Peters, how do you respond to the contention
by your adversary that prohibiting marijuana,
while allowing legal access to alcohol, deprives
those who seek the marijuana route to pleasure
equal protection of the laws?

MR. PETERS:
I touched on this a bit earlier. First of all, as the

American Medical Association and the National
Academy of Sciences have noted, the comparison
between alcohol and marijuana is not valid. When
people say that marijuana is less dangerous than
alcohol, they are comparing the relatively mild
effects of moderate marijuana use with the destructive effects of chronic alcoholism. Chronic marijuana use is very destructive, as the experience in
India, Morocco, and Egypt, as well as in some of our
mental hospitals, indicates.

But equally significant, there is no constitutional
compulsion for the legislature to prohibit all harmful substances or none at all. Each prohibition has
to be looked at on its own merits.

My opponent bases much of his argument on the
fact that moderate use of marijuana will not adversely affect the stable, well-adjusted person. Society, and therefore the law, has to take into
account, however, the adverse consequences that
would result if marijuana were made readily available to the millions of persons who are not stable,
those who are predisposed to impulsive and aggressive behavior, persons who can't cope with the
mind-altering qualities of this potentially very dangerous drug.

Now certainly alcohol is a highly destructive
substance that harms both the individual drinker
and society. So is tobacco, and so are a number
of other substances that are freely used by people.
But to argue that because we may have roaches in
our home, we should bring the rats in I think
misses the point. It is always harder to prohibit

something that has been in general and mostly unrestricted use than it is to keep something that has always been suspected as being dangerous on the restricted list. I think our experience with Prohibition in the twenties proved that. The mere fact that we are forced by circumstances of politics to allow the sale of some harmful substances does not mean that additional harmful substances should now be turned loose.

We just don't know enough about marijuana to give it a clean bill of health. Many nations have sought to prohibit its use, and I think this is at least indicative that it is not as harmless as some people say. In 1967, an article was published in an educational journal. Its author was probably a well-meaning young man who espoused the liberal ideology that is currently so popular. He wrote, "Since marijuana is essentially harmless, although more research is badly needed, and it appears that safe consumption of LSD is possible for most people, the spread of their use should not be a cause for alarm. . . . I would argue therefore for the legalization of both marijuana and LSD and would hope that their use be constrained only insofar as the still lacking scientific evidence of danger dictates." Science and many deformed or aborted babies have proved him wrong about LSD; the full returns are not yet in for marijuana. However, as I have already indicated, we do know enough about marijuana to say that it can be very dangerous indeed.

I think that Dr. James L. Goddard, the former

director of the U.S. Food and Drug Administration, put it very well when he responded to the often asked question of why, if the known dangers of alcohol and tobacco are greater than the known dangers of marijuana, we shouldn't legalize marijuana. He said, "I believe that if alcohol and tobacco were not already legal, we might very well decide not to legalize them—knowing what we now know. In the case of marijuana, we will know in a very few years how harmful it is or is not. If it turns out to be relatively harmless, we will be embarrassed by harsh laws that made innocent people suffer. If it turns out to be quite harmful—a distinct possibility—we will have introduced yet another public health hazard that for social and economic reasons might become impossible to dislodge."

I respectfully submit that even what we now know is sufficient to sustain the laws prohibiting the possession and sale of marijuana and that Rodriguez' conviction should be affirmed.

PART FOUR

Rebuttal on Behalf of
Peter Rodriguez

THE CHIEF JUSTICE:

Mr. Smith, do you have any rebuttal?

MR. SMITH:

I do, Mr. Chief Justice. I am absolutely amazed at the mass of scare statistics and unreliable reports that has been presented this morning.

Now, as has already been pointed out, marijuana is only one of the substances which can be obtained from the female hemp or *Cannabis* plant. In addition, science has extracted and synthesized the chemical substance thought to be responsible for marijuana's intoxicating qualities. This substance, known as THC, is more than one hundred times as powerful as the marijuana commonly smoked in the United States. Most of the adverse effects that my opponent has blamed on marijuana are, in truth, attributable to either hashish, which is, as I have noted, the concentrated resin from the flowering tops of the female hemp plant and is up to six times more powerful than marijuana, or THC. Because hashish and THC are more potent than marijuana, it is not surprising that they produce different results. It would make as much sense to blame beer for the evils of distilled liquor.

In addition, some of the experimenters have been assuming that they can accurately determine the properties of a substance by increasing its potency or dosage until some reaction is observed. This, of course, is utter nonsense. You cannot administer huge doses of THC to a subject and then, when he develops adverse reactions, say: "Look at what marijuana can do!" To ban marijuana on the basis of these experiments would be as logical as to ban the household cooking spice, nutmeg, merely because, for example, a person who eats one ounce of powdered nutmeg will become euphoric, will see hallucinations, and will sometimes suffer from delirium and physical collapse.

MR. JUSTICE BADGER:

How much nutmeg is one ounce?

MR. SMITH:

Four to six nutmegs, Your Honor. The answer is, of course, that too much of anything is, by definition, no good. My adversary has continuously been guilty of trying to saddle marijuana with the results of experiments that have no relation to the way marijuana is commonly smoked in this country.

MR. JUSTICE STANBERY:

In what way?

MR. SMITH:

Take, for example, his conclusion that in high enough quantities marijuana can produce a psychotic reaction in just about everyone. This was based on Dr. Isbell's experiments with THC. We have no quarrel with his conclusion that overdoses of THC are dangerous; we submit, however, that it is irrelevant to the question of whether marijuana, in standardized and regulated strengths, is dangerous enough to warrant making its possession criminal.

My adversary's reliance upon the finding of the LaGuardia committee that, given the correct environment and personality of the user, marijuana can produce "a true psychotic state" is also misplaced. First of all, the LaGuardia committee researchers recognized that the person who smokes marijuana is able to control his dosage in order to achieve the most pleasurable sensations. Stated another way, the individual will smoke only as much marijuana as is necessary. He will not overindulge. Precise control is possible because when a marijuana cigarette is smoked, its effects come on very rapidly. In order to bypass this self-regulating feature, what the scientists call "self-titration," the LaGuardia committee prepared a concentrated marijuana extract and gave it to the subjects in pill form. Thus, not only was the subjects' ability to regulate their own dosage bypassed, but the nature of the substance was altered.

The LaGuardia committee recognized that the process of combustion—which occurs when marijuana is smoked—probably alters the effect of the chemicals that are absorbed by the body. Additionally, when the extract is swallowed, it is acted upon by the body's digestive tract, while the marijuana passes directly into the bloodstream when its smoke is inhaled into the lungs. The LaGuardia committee emphasized that these were vital differences, for they noted that when the marijuana was smoked, "the main effect was of a euphoric type" and that the "condition described as 'high' came on promptly and increased with the number of cigarettes smoked, but it was not alarming or definitely disagreeable, and did not give rise to anti-social behavior. On the contrary, it prompted sociability. The marijuana was under the subject's control, and once the euphoric state was present, which might come from only one cigarette, he had no inclination to increase it by more smoking. When a considerable number of cigarettes were smoked, the effect was usually one of drowsiness and fatigue."

This is to be contrasted with the result when the marijuana concentrate was in pill form. The researchers noted that the "subject's consciousness of unpleasant symptoms" was "more marked" and that the "long duration of action and the inability of the subject to stop it" served "to accentuate the physical symptoms and to cause apprehension." They further noted that the "result of all this readily accounts for the irritability, negativism and antagonism" that they saw when the concentrate was administered.

Now, not only was a concentrate used, but, as I noted in my main argument, it was given to subjects who were drawn from New York City prisons. Those who suffered adverse reactions from the concentrate had histories of severe mental problems. In fact, the researchers attributed one of the adverse reactions to plain and simple prison psychosis. After reviewing the results of the experiment, the commissioner of correction for New York City commented that he was surprised that the subjects were so little trouble. He noted that, in words I quoted earlier, "the few psychotic episodes that occurred are exactly what we would expect in the whole group without considering the administration and effects of excessive doses of marijuana."

In sum, this portion of the LaGuardia committee experiments proved only that if you make volunteer prisoners swallow huge and excessive doses of a marijuana extract, you can expect to get some adverse reactions, especially in those with histories of psychological problems. The experiment was obviously designed to test the upper limits of marijuana's effect on human beings and is irrelevant to a determination of how marijuana, as it is commonly smoked in this country, affects the general population. As Dr. Zinberg noted, psychotic reactions caused by smoking marijuana are so rare as to be classified as "psychiatric curiosities."

My adversary also mentioned Dr. Keeler's interviews with people who had unpleasant experiences with marijuana—well, they couldn't have been too unpleasant because nine out of the eleven he interviewed continued to smoke marijuana. Also, the studies of soldiers who have used marijuana in Vietnam are misleading. The Vietnam war zone is an area of exceedingly high stress, and the reactions observed there cannot be related to marijuana use here. Significantly, the Army psychiatrists report that the soldiers' symptoms subsided when they were given the "water treatment," that is, when they were flown across the ocean and returned to the United States.

Now much of my opponent's argument this morning was based on reports from India, Morocco, and the like. These reports are notoriously unreliable. Aside from the fact that the substance used is, more often than not, hashish, there are other factors present that obscure any result. Primarily, there is no accurate way of determining that the adverse effects noted were actually caused by cannabis. They could have been caused by such diverse factors as malnutrition, the individual's own susceptibility to emotional problems, and the general environment. I therefore agree with Dr. Zinberg that observations of the effects of hemp as it is used abroad "simply have no relevance to the situation in our country." It should be noted, however, that the Indian Hemp Drugs Commission—in an extensive study and report—concluded that moderate use of hemp produces no ill effects and that, aside from what they call "the most exceptional cases," moderate habitual use is not harmful. The LaGuardia committee researchers, in their extensive study of chronic marijuana users, also noted that marijuana use does not cause mental or physical deterioration.

Marijuana has been smoked in this country for nearly fifty years. Every study has shown that it is not harmful except in very limited and unusual circumstances. The plain and simple fact is that marijuana, as it is smoked in this country, is not dangerous. It is far less dangerous to society and to the user than either alcohol or tobacco. Millions of respectable Americans smoke and enjoy marijuana and suffer no ill effects. They know it is not dangerous, and have emphasized this by their willingness to risk harsh criminal penalties to enjoy its sensations.

MR. JUSTICE BADGER:
How do you answer your adversary's charge that marijuana use can lead to sexual perversion?

MR. SMITH:
I was a bit surprised at that one, Your Honor. I thought that such charges against marijuana went out of style long ago. First, marijuana, like alcohol, does tend to lower inhibitions. In that respect some people may use it to facilitate their doing things which they would not ordinarily do. But alcohol is used much more extensively for this purpose. There is nothing in the properties of marijuana that can cause lust. In fact, while it is true that some people in India will try cannabis because they erroneously think that it can improve their sex lives, India's holy men also take cannabis to suppress their bodies' natural sexual urges. It seems that marijuana in this regard is like Al Capp's shmoo—it is what you want it to be.

Secondly, all those wild parties which supposedly took place while everyone was high on marijuana appear to me to be something which the servicemen made up to con, or have fun with, what appeared to them to be a bunch of nosy psychiatrists. In any event, the wild sex orgies supposedly took place in New York at the same time that the LaGuardia committee was making its in-the-field investigations. The investigators found no such activity and reported, to the contrary, that marijuana was not used as an adjunct to sexual activity.

Additionally, as I have pointed out in my main argument, there is absolutely no evidence that marijuana causes crime or that it leads to narcotic addiction. There is no evidence at all that marijuana will adversely affect the overwhelmingly vast majority of people.

MR. JUSTICE PECKHAM:

What about the others—isn't protection of those who might be harmed by marijuana sufficient justification for the legislature to ban it?

MR. SMITH:

There is absolutely no evidence that moderate use of marijuana causes harm. Some people have suffered adverse psychological reactions coincidental with marijuana use, but the cause and effect relationship has not been established. As has been noted, marijuana's effect is largely dependent upon the personality of the user. It will not cause a normal person to become abnormal. In a free society, people have the right to decide for themselves how they will seek their pleasure. If no one is harmed, the government may not interfere with that choice.

THE CHIEF JUSTICE:

What about the very serious charge that marijuana can cause birth defects?

MR. SMITH:

I'm glad you asked that, Mr. Chief Justice, because I was just about to touch on it.

Marijuana has been used for five thousand years —in some countries hashish is smoked in huge amounts—and birth defects attributable to cannabis have not been observed anywhere. Secondly, many substances that are harmless in man are teratogenic in some animals. Insulin, penicillin, and even aspirin all can cause fetal malformations in animals. There is no evidence at all that marijuana can cause birth defects in human beings.

In sum, then, we submit that it has not been demonstrated that marijuana is harmful to the user or dangerous to society, and therefore we maintain that government cannot prohibit its use.

MR. JUSTICE BRADFORD:

There is still one thing I don't understand: if marijuana is as innocuous as you say, why has it been banned in most countries, especially those countries which have long histories of alcohol consumption?

MR. SMITH:

In Western culture, where the Protestant work ethic predominates, inaction and introspection are suspected and feared. Any substance that produces inaction and introspection is also suspected and feared. This is not true in the East, and cannabis is a socially acceptable product in Eastern countries. On the other hand, alcohol tends to induce activity and aggression and therefore fits in with

149

the Western idea of acceptable social behavior. It is interesting to note that in Eastern countries, where aggression and activity are not part of the culture, alcohol is decidedly less popular than cannabis. But this difference in cultures certainly is not a valid reason to prohibit marijuana.

Marijuana is not a dangerous drug, and people should have a right to use it if they want to. If the Constitution means anything, it means that people have a fundamental right to decide things for themselves—they have, in short, a right to be let alone. Thus, we submit that while marijuana, like alcohol, can be regulated, it cannot be prohibited. Certainly there is no compelling social reason to make criminal its private possession. In fact, an interdepartmental Health, Education, and Welfare memorandum in 1967 recommended that criminal penalties for the private and personal possession of marijuana be repealed. Although for various political reasons this never became official policy, it does indicate that at least some government scientists recognize that marijuana is not as dangerous as some would have us believe.

THE CHIEF JUSTICE:

How realistic is it, however, to assume that if we do say that the private possession and use of marijuana is beyond the reach of governmental prohibition, regulation will be any more successful with marijuana than it has been with alcohol?

MR. SMITH:

Obviously, we can't be sure that governmental regulation will be 100 percent effective. I suppose that there always will be an underground traffic in harmful drugs just as there is now. But what legalization will do is ensure that those people who do use marijuana will be using a standardized product. Additionally, just as alcoholic consumption increased during Prohibition, undoubtedly there are people who smoke marijuana precisely because it is illegal. If marijuana is legalized, there is a likelihood that its use will level off.

As this Court said in the Georgia pornography case, the way to deal with collateral problems of private possession of pornography is through education and the deterrent effect of criminal punishment. So it is with whatever the collateral problems of legalized marijuana may be. The existence of these collateral problems, however, is no reason for the government to prohibit the private possession of marijuana any more than the existence of collateral problems with respect to obscenity is any reason for the government to prohibit its private possession. The laws against marijuana, although postured as attempts to prevent harm to persons and to society, are really attempts at imposing legislatively determined morality upon the individual. The Constitution, however, stands as a bar and the laws are invalid.

In conclusion, let me quote from what I feel is one of the best statements of our basic position. It was written over sixty years ago by Judge Henry Barker of the Court of Appeals of Kentucky in the case of *Commonwealth* v. *Campbell*. The issue was whether the legislature could prohibit the possession of liquor for private consumption. The court said no—and Judge Barker wrote:

The Bill of Rights, which declares that among the inalienable rights possessed by the citizens is that of seeking and pursuing their safety and happiness, and that the absolute and arbitrary power over the lives, liberty, and property of free-man exists nowhere in a republic, not even in the largest majority, would be but an empty sound if the Legislature could prohibit the citizen the right of owning or drinking liquor, when in so doing he did not offend the laws of decency by being intoxicated in public. Man in his natural state has a right to do whatever he chooses and has the power to do. When he becomes a member of organized society, under governmental regulation, he surrenders, of necessity, all of his natural right, the exercise of which is, or may be injurious to his fellow citizens. This is the price that he pays for governmental protection, but it is not within the competency of a free government to invade the sanctity of the absolute rights of the citizen any further than the direct protection of society requires. Therefore the question of what a man will drink, or eat, or own, provided the rights of others are not invaded, is one which addresses itself alone to the will of the citizen. It is not within the competency of government to invade the privacy of a citizen's life and to regulate his conduct in matters in which he alone is concerned, or to prohibit him any liberty the exercise of which will not directly injure society.

The judge noted that while the state could regulate the sale of liquor, it could not ban personal possession. He found that the "right to use liquor for one's own comfort, if the use is without direct injury to the public, is one of the citizen's natural and inalienable rights, guaranteed to him by the Constitution, and cannot be abridged as long as the absolute power of a majority is limited by our present constitution." I am well aware that several years after this was written this Court upheld laws outlawing the private possession of alcohol, but I respectfully submit that it should reconsider. I call upon the Court to reaffirm the right of man to choose his own destiny. Rodriguez' conviction should be reversed.

THE CHIEF JUSTICE:
Thank you, gentlemen, for your submission. The case will stand submitted.

Author's Postscript

Rodriguez v. *Pennsylvania* has been argued, and the Court has taken the case under submission. The Supreme Court usually announces its decision one to two months after oral argument. Although, as an attorney, I was tempted to carry this fiction one step further and to decide this case according to my view of the law, I resisted the temptation. The main purpose of this book is to explore the marijuana controversy and not to provide answers in the form of a pronunciamento.

Ultimately, the decision as to whether marijuana should be legalized depends on the attitudes of the entire citizenry. Our legislators and judges are more or less sensitive and responsive to the changing needs of society. As our experience with Prohibition proved, laws cannot endure that are imposed from above. Rather, they must spring from a sense of justice—what is right—that is shared by all.

If, after all the facts are known and aired, we still think marijuana to be a dangerous drug, it will continue to be outlawed. However, if a great many people feel that its alleged dangers are outweighed by its alleged benefits, it will be legalized. For in the final analysis, law must serve the society which formulates its principles and cannot remain static. Thus, the highest court in the land, in the words of Henry Steele Commager, must contribute "resourcefulness and imagination—the resourcefulness to find in the elusive phrases of the Constitution authority for making it an instrument rather than a limitation, and the imagination to foresee the direction which the law and the Constitution must take if the Constitution, and the nation, are to 'endure for ages to come.'"